I've A Sto

Stories of Inspiration in an Ordinary Life

Judy Williams

I've a Story to Tell

ISBN 978-0-9833643-1-3

cover and interior design Dekie Hicks
illustrations by Bob Mulford

WP
wheredepony
Wheredepony Press
Rome, GA 30165
www.wheredeponypress.com
printed in the United States of America

I dedicate this book to my husband Jimmy,
my very own Southern gentleman

Table of Contents

Acknowledgments

I never set out to write stories. I consider myself a story *teller* not a story *writer*. In over thirty years of teaching Bible studies and Sunday school classes and speaking before groups I have told stories to make pertinent points. I have always been amazed at how God has inspired me with memories and experiences which developed into a narrative and brought a completion to every lesson. My Heavenly Father is truly the Inspirer of every story that I write and tell.

God has blessed me with my wonderful husband Jimmy who has not only been a source for many of my stories, he is also my greatest supporter, encourager and critic. I appreciate—more than he can ever know—his patience with me. There have been many times he has listened to a story over and over again until I felt it was exactly as God wanted it to be told.

My friends and family are not only instrumental in teaching me the ways of God, many times they have not even realized the important lessons I have learned from them. Their presence in my life and their interaction with me have helped me grow in my spiritual walk. Without their love and friendship I would be a very lonely person.

The Gatekeepers Sunday School Class of Tuckston United Methodist Church has been my sounding board. Not only have they heard hundreds of my stories, they always express their appreciation for the lessons I teach in such gracious ways. It is from this class that I first received encouragement to put pen to paper and write this account. Despite my initial misgivings, it is through the persistence and encouragement of my family, friends, and my Sunday school class that this collection of stories has materialized.

Two members of the Gatekeepers Class in particular have been my most stalwart encouragers and supporters. Barbara Cornelius, the author of *Lazarus Still Rises* and *God's Postmarks*, has been a wonderful advisor. Without her optimistic reassurance, this book would still be in my head. Bob Mulford created the drawings which so beautifully illustrate the subject matter of each section. Thank you to Barbara and Bob for helping me finish this work of my heart.

Dekie Hicks, my copy editor, has removed commas, added periods or dashes and made other grammatical corrections to make this narrative more readable and understandable. I love the way she laughs at my humorous stories. Dekie has worked tirelessly to help bring my book to completion and for her efforts I will be forever grateful.

The Purpose of My Stories

Dear Reader,

It is so amazing for me to see God at work in every moment of my life. Or may I more accurately say, it is so amazing to me that I have the potential to see God at work in every moment of my life. When I keep my focus on God, He reveals Himself to me.

The following stories help to illustrate the many ways I have become aware of my loving Heavenly Father in the everydayness of my life on this earth. He began to reveal Himself to me before I was even aware of Him. As I look back on my childhood experiences, I can see Him at work in my early years, in my teenage years, in my young adulthood, and, most of all now in my grown up years.

I began this work of my heart by retelling stories I sometimes have been told and have now been made a part of my memory. These stories prepared the way for my awakening to the love of God. As the stories progress, I begin to illustrate how I see and experience God in my daily life—through experiences both happy and sad, through common daily chores or events, through friends and loved ones and their interactions with me and others, through inspiration and memories.

My hope for anyone who reads these stories is that you also may begin to look for and see how very alive our God is and how very much He wants to reveal Himself to you in the ordinariness of what you do every day. In Deuteronomy 31:6, He has promised that "He will never leave (us) or forsake (us)", and He keeps His promises.

I serve a risen Savior, He's in the world today.
I know that He is living, whatever men may say.
I see His hand of mercy, I hear His voice of cheer,
And, every time I need Him, He's always near.
He lives, He lives, Christ Jesus lives today.
He walks with me and talks with me along life's narrow way.
He lives, He lives, salvation to impart.
You ask me how I know He lives: He lives within my heart!

Judy Williams
September, 2014

Introduction

I was born with an identical twin, Julie, and we had an amazing childhood. It was so much fun being twins. Not only did we look alike but we also dressed alike most of our growing-up years. We loved to fool people and get them mixed up about us, and we must have gotten this teasing nature from our Dad, who was the biggest teaser of all.

One day, however, his teasing had a profound effect on me. I was very young when, in his kidding manner, he said to me, "Judy, you know what? I think your mother and I got you and Julie mixed up on the day you were born. I think you might be Julie." I knew Daddy was teasing. I could hear the lightheartedness in his voice, but this thought entered my mind and sunk into some deep recesses: what if I weren't "me"! My young mind didn't see this confusion as just being a mix-up of the "name." It was a mix-up of the "being." I did not want to be someone else! I wanted to be ME!

As I grew into adulthood, I knew I was Judy, but I certainly did not know WHO I was. It was years later before I learned and came to believe I am a child of God. I belong to Him. Philippians 1:6: "I am confident of this, that He who began a good work in you will carry it on to completion until the day of Christ Jesus." God began His work, His good work, in me long before I recognized Him. Every day I learn more about who I am and more about the One to Whom I belong.

One day many years later, when I was "all grown up" and had children of my own, I mentioned the above incident to my daddy. "Judy," he said, "I've thought about that occasion when I teased you with that statement many times over the years, and I am so sorry I said that to you. It was an awful thing to say to a child. Will you forgive me?" Of course there was nothing to forgive. I had sorted it all out many years before. I am Judy, and I belong to Jesus.

Part I

PREPARING THE WAY

I am confident of this: God loves every one of His children, so much so that He puts things and people in our paths to help us turn to Him, to help us recognize Him, to help us grow in Him. The stories I am about to tell reveal some of the incidents that have pointed me to the way of Jesus, have helped me grow into His likeness. He does this amazing work in us even before we have an inkling of His existence. He loves us so much that He sent His only Son to bring us home. He has prepared my way.

*The promise is for you and your children
and for all who are far off –
for all whom the Lord our God will call.*

Acts 2:39

CHAPTER ONE

Great Granddaddy Thomas
God Had a Plan

James Jackson Thomas and Mary Ann Evans, my great grandparents, were married in the mid 1850s. Within a few years, they had a small house and farm in south Georgia and it was not long before they had three sons. The Civil War broke out, and James was drafted to fight for the Confederacy. For most of the war, James was stationed near the Mason-Dixon Line, where some of the heaviest and most brutal battles were fought. Mary Ann stayed at home in the South to take care of the farm and their family.

The years passed, and although the battlefront was difficult, with the constant lack of food and shelter, death and injury of friends and fellow soldiers, discouragement, and the constant fear of injury and death, life on the farm with small children and no husband was also difficult. Mary Ann was a trooper. She kept the farm going even as the days and years passed. The letters from

James became more and more infrequent. He didn't tell her that he had been injured and that one of his legs had been amputated.

April, 1865, the war between the North and the South ended. The South and the Confederacy were devastated, and the defeated soldiers began to make their way back to their homes and farms. James began the journey, walking many miles to south Georgia with only one leg. The trip was long and arduous, but he finally approached the outskirts of the farm he had left several years before. Although his heart must have been rejoicing at finally reaching his destination, I imagine he felt discouraged, anxious and worried about his family and how they had fared during the war as he traveled the dusty road leading to his home. He saw fences that needed mending, a weed-filled garden with little produce in it, nothing growing in the fields.

As this scraggly, skinny, unkempt, one-legged man drew within sight of his once familiar farmhouse, he saw Mary Ann and their sons on the porch. But, Mary Ann held a shotgun in her hands and the gun was pointed at him! James tried to convince Mary Ann that he was her husband, but the man standing before her looked nothing like the young, polished, healthy, robust man who had left her four years earlier.

Finally, Mary Ann allowed the boys—shotgun in hand—to escort this stranger to the creek so he could wash up, shave, and then come back and let her have another look. When they returned to the house, Mary Ann was still not fully convinced this was her man, but she allowed him to come into the house anyway. Of course, he ended up staying, and that's a good thing, because my grandfather, Thomas Jefferson Thomas, was born a few years later. In fact, the family of James and Mary Ann Thomas grew from the original three children to twelve—ten boys and two girls.

God began planning for me and for my future many generations ago, even before James and Mary Ann got married. He had plans for me when he brought my great granddaddy home to the devastated South and he and my great grandmother rebuilt their lives teaching their children to not only work hard but to always trust in God. God's plans and hope

begin for us even before we are "knit together in our mother's womb." (Psalm 139:13) He has a plan for every one of his children, a plan to prosper each of us and not to harm us, a plan to give us a future and a hope. (Jeremiah 29:13).

*Yet this I call to mind and therefore I have hope:
because of the Lord's great love we are not consumed,
for his compassions never fail.
They are new every morning;
great is your faithfulness.*

Lamentations 3:21-23

CHAPTER TWO

Lorene

A Courageous Woman Walks The Path Of Life

*I*grew up in a small town in the days before televisions, iPads, smart phones even computers! I grew up in a time when neighbors visited…and friends came over…and relatives stopped by…and we were entertained by listening to and telling stories. I was always very impressed by the stories told of a particular lady who had grown up in my hometown. My ears perked up when I heard her name, and I paid particular attention to all the stories told about Lorene. She was born in 1916. Her daddy was a railroad engineer and her mother stayed at home, as most mothers did in those days, raising Lorene and her older brother. Often her mother played the piano at the church they attended.

Of the two children, Lorene was the precocious one—very active, very inquisitive, energetic and vivacious…and very charming. She made friends easily and quickly—long lasting friends who would be faithful to each other all their lives. Lorene was also a very beautiful girl.

Growing up during the "Roaring 20s," Lorene was a child of her time. Just say "party" or "dance" and she was the first one there with all her friends, both boys and girls, all of them partying and dancing with each other.

The years passed and the friendships strengthened and grew. But when high school graduation came, everyone knew it was time to go their separate ways. Some would remain in town to attend the local college, some would leave for distant colleges, some would marry. Lorene's very best friend, Beth, married and moved to Orangeburg, SC. These two girls missed each other. They would write letters to each other, occasionally talk by phone, and sometimes they would visit each other. On one of her visits to Orangeburg, Lorene met a young man, and during the months that followed, through visits, letters and calls, Lorene and the young man fell in love.

Their love became serious and they began to talk about getting married. One weekend as she was preparing to go visit, she felt they would become engaged. She and a friend would be driving together.

No one knows exactly what happened, but just outside Orangeburg, a head-on collision occurred. Those were the days before seat belts, before windshields were made of tempered glass, the days when hoods of cars folded up accordion style upon impact. The driver of the car was uninjured, but Lorene was thrown head and shoulders through the plate glass windshield, her face slamming into the accordion folded hood of the car.

She was rushed to the hospital in Orangeburg where the doctors fought to save her life. She had multiple broken bones, lacerations and contusions, but her most extensive injuries were to her face and head. The right side of her face was crushed. Her right eye had been gouged out.

Lorene loved life. She loved people, and she had a lot to live for. She began a long, slow recovery. During the many weeks she was hospitalized, her young man came to see her every day. He brought her flowers and candy. He sat and held her hand and encouraged her. A few days before she was to be discharged, he came to see her one last time. He came to tell her he could not marry her because he could not endure looking at her scarred and crushed face for the rest of his life.

Lorene returned to her hometown, to the love and support of her family and her friends, to the fellowship and love of her church. She earned a teaching degree at the local college and began to teach second grade.

A year or two passed, and one day she met a young man from Mississippi named Flournoy. Lorene and Flournoy began to date…and they fell in love. This was not a shallow, superficial love, but an enduring, forever-after love. In May of 1939, Lorene and Flournoy were married. Several years passed and children came along. The children were raised in the church, learning of the love of God from an early age. Lorene and Flournoy taught their girls to kneel by their beds at night and pray. They read the Bible with them and took them to Sunday school and church to learn of the ways of God.

In the 16th chapter of the Gospel of John, Jesus is talking to His disciples about what is about to happen to Him, telling them the things they are about to face. Jesus doesn't want them to be fearful and He says to them, "I'm telling you these things so that you will have peace. In this world you will have tribulation, but don't be afraid, I have overcome the world."

"In this world you will have tribulation." Has ever a truer statement been made? In this world we *will* have tragedy, heartache, grief, rejection, pain. During these times of tribulation we, all of us, make the choice of how we will respond. Will we turn to the One who has promised He has overcome the world or will we turn away from Him? Will we embrace His truth, His promises… or will we reject Him? Will we grow in our faith or…will we lose our faith?

I believe our Heavenly Father hurts when we hurt (He hurt when Lorene was thrown through that windshield). He weeps with us when we weep (He wept with Lorene when her young man turned away from her. He wept when she experienced rejection, because He has known rejection, too). He rejoices with us and He celebrates with us (as He did when Lorene and Flournoy found love together). In this world we will have tribulation, but do not fear, our God has overcome the world.

Lorene's young man from South Carolina made a choice after her accident. He turned away. Lorene also made a choice. She chose to move forward in the strength of God. She chose to allow Him to be her courage to face the future. She chose to allow God to bring her comfort and to heal the brokenness of her body and her spirit. She chose to move toward God into the hope and the future He promised her. She chose God, and He blessed her.

Lorene was blessed and she was a blessing to all who knew her throughout her life: her friends, her family, her husband, her daughters. She was a blessing to me. Lorene was my mother. Lorene and Flournoy, my parents, were married for over fifty years and they told each other they loved each other every single day of their lives together.

I have been blessed to be touched and inspired by this Godly woman. Just as I have been blessed, may God empower me to be a blessing to others. And to Him be the glory.

Judy Williams

> *But while he was still a long way off,*
> *His father saw him and was filled with compassion for him; He ran to*
> *his son, threw his arms around him, and kissed him.*
>
> **Luke 15:20**

CHAPTER THREE

The Babies

Love Is Always Waiting

My sister and I were so blessed to grow up near our grandparents. We saw them often. As our car would turn the corner to 404 E. Rogers Street, Julie and I could see Granny and Granddaddy sitting on the big old gray wooden porch in the rocking chairs Granddaddy had made. As we turned into the driveway, I could see his grin, spread from ear to ear.

When the car finally stopped in the driveway, we could hardly get the door open quickly enough. Then, running as fast as our little legs would carry us up the stairs, we jumped into Granddaddy's wide-open arms and onto his lap. We jumped into Granddaddy's lap because Granny didn't have a lap, if you know what I mean! "Well, look who came to see us, Granny," he would turn to my Granny and say. "The babies." That's what he always called me and Julie...the babies.

With Granddaddy's arms wrapped around me, I felt the warmth

of his love enclosing every cell of my body. I knew I was safe as he held me. I could see his love for me in his eyes, hear it in his voice, feel it in his touch. On days we didn't get to go over to our grandparents' house, I missed the love and security, and I missed his attentiveness to all my childish statements.

And he, too, missed our visits. He missed wrapping his arms around us, hearing about our "adventures," and listening to our questions. I know he missed us because Granny told me that on days we did not go to see them, he would question her, "Well, Granny, I wonder where the babies were today?" He looked forward to our coming to see him just as much as we looked forward to visiting him.

I believe our Heavenly Father is like Granddaddy in that way. I believe He waits longingly for each one of us to come visit Him each day…I believe He waits for us with open arms… I believe He waits to hear about what we have been doing, where we have been or plan to go, what makes us sad or happy. I believe He waits to whisper to us words of comfort and love, and He wants to remove fear far from us in the warmth of His embrace. I believe He wants to listen to us as we express our fears, concerns, hopes, dreams, and He wants to speak to us about each one.

On days we do not come to visit Him, I can hear our Heavenly Father say, "Well, Jesus, I wonder where the babies were today." On those days we do not visit our Heavenly Father, He misses us as much as we miss being in His presence.

Judy Williams

This is the day the Lord has made;
let us rejoice and be glad in it.

Psalm 118:24

CHAPTER FOUR

Daddy and the Switch

The Turn-Around Of Life

Sometimes God just asks us to sit down and wait on Him. Sometimes He just wants us to open our eyes of faith to the hope and the future He has for us.

One day when my Daddy (Flournoy) was a little boy, he was taking a walk in the woods with his Daddy (Granddaddy Vinson). Taking walks with his daddy was a favorite pastime of Flournoy's. He had three sisters, and anytime he could get away from them and out of the house with his daddy was a great treat.

It was a beautiful fall day: crisp, cool air and colorful, crackling leaves underfoot. Of course, Flournoy ran on ahead, playing cowboys and Indians and hiding behind every tree and boulder along the path. He and his daddy walked and whistled and played and enjoyed each other and their time together.

Finally, his daddy told Flournoy it was time to turn around and head back home. Flournoy wasn't ready to go. He pouted and he frowned and he mumbled and grumbled. But Granddaddy Vinson insisted, and they turned around. Now Flournoy wasn't running ahead, he was lagging behind, dragging his feet, mumbling and grumbling and fussing. Granddaddy Vinson took Flournoy's "attitude" as long as he could then he said, "Flournoy, sit down on that rock." Flournoy sat down and watched as his daddy walked over to a Hickory tree and cut a long "switch."

Flournoy's eyes got bigger and bigger as he watched his daddy smooth up that switch and get all the little nubs off it. "Why didn't I keep my mouth shut? Why didn't I just behave? Now look what's going to happen!" All these thoughts were running through his head. Finally, Granddaddy Vinson finished polishing the switch and walked toward Flournoy who was trying to make himself invisible.

Granddaddy Vinson walked straight up to Flournoy, thrust the "switch" out to him, and said, "Now, Flournoy, throw your leg over that horse and ride him home." Wow! For Flournoy a new adventure began on the walk home, an adventure even better than the beginning of the trip as that horse galloped and jumped and wove in and out of the forest to blaze a new trail back to the "ranch."

Flournoy thought the first part of the day was the best and really regretted having to turn around to come home, but his vision, his outlook on "life," changed when his father showed him that the real adventure was ahead, a new and exciting ride. I thought my life was wonderful and full before I became a Christian. Now, as I look at things through the eyes of God, I see my real life began the day I accepted Jesus as my Lord and Savior.

Judy Williams

> *The Lord will watch over your coming and going,*
> *both now and forevermore.*
>
> **Psalm 121:8**

CHAPTER FIVE

The Bobbsey Twins
Living In Crisis

*E*very night before my sister and I would go to bed, our daddy would sit between us and read a story. This was my favorite time of the day because Daddy was an extremely gifted storyteller. Some of our favorite books were those about the Bobbsey Twins. The Bobbseys were a family who had two sets of twins. The older twins were Nan and Bert, and the younger twins were Flossie and Freddie.

The twins had all kinds of adventures and experiences as characters of this type generally do. The younger twins had a nemesis in their neighborhood. An older boy named Danny, who was about the age of Nan and Bert, seemed to have made it his life's goal to antagonize Flossie and Freddie. Danny loved to get the younger twins in trouble.

The exciting thing about these stories of the Bobbsey twins was that the reader (or listener in our case) was left hanging at the end of each chapter. The younger twins, and sometimes the older twins, were in some kind of crisis situation: they were lost, they were in trouble or about to be in trouble, they were being blamed for something they had not done, etc. You had to read the next chapter to know if the twins were safe, or if the real culprit had been found, or how they were going to get out of the situation in which they found themselves. Of course, Daddy built up the end of each chapter so much that Julie and I could hardly wait until the next night to see how the twins got out of whatever predicament they were in. The anticipation was so strong it was almost tangible.

I don't remember any specific antics the twins got into or any specific adventure they had, but I do remember my Daddy sitting beside me every night, reading to me, spending time with me. Time, to a child, is precious. Time is the special ingredient of memories.

I remember the times my Heavenly Father has sat with me when I was anticipating, or anxious, or sad, times when I didn't know what the next day would bring and my anxious thoughts multiplied within me. His very presence was just what I needed...His time with me, my time with Him.

Judy Williams

A new command I give you: Love one another.
As I have loved you, so you must love one another.
By this all men will know that you are my disciples,
if you love one another.

John 13: 34,35

CHAPTER SIX

Living Love

Granddaddy "Lived" Love

Although Granddaddy Thomas died when I was ten years old, he had a profound impact on my life. In a previous story, "The Babies," I tell about how he helped me to learn the importance of "visiting" my Heavenly Father regularly. This story relates how Granddaddy helped me learn about living a life in relationship with God.

When we would visit Granddaddy's house, and sit on his knees —one knee for Julie and one knee for me—he would wrap his arms around us, his sweet pipe breath on our faces. After a few minutes we would look intently at him and he would cut his eyes toward his bedroom. We knew what that meant…in his bedroom, in a drawer beside his bed, was some chewing gum for us—Juicy Fruit, our favorite! We would jump down from his lap and run to get our treat.

Summers found my sister and me sitting for hours on stumps in Granddaddy's back yard, chewing sugar cane that he carefully peeled and cut into bite size pieces for us. Sometimes we would chew a piece for only a few seconds before spitting it out and holding out our hand for the next piece. Granddaddy's patience was unlimited; he would peel sugar cane for us as long as we would chew it.

He had a little carpenter's shop off the garage in the back yard and we loved to go in there and smell the wood shavings, see the fresh planed wood, and ask him about what he was building now. From this little shop he built doll strollers for us, a small glider set which just fit Julie and me, and stilts which he taught us by example how to walk on.

In the winter in front of the big coal fire in his living room he would peel oranges for each one of us, getting all the skin off so we wouldn't have chapped lips. Then he would cut out a little core, squeeze the oranges until they were really juicy and hand one to each of us. We would suck those oranges dry! Sometimes he would hand one of us the tongs to place a big piece of black, shiny, lump coal on the fire and watch it blaze up the old brick chimney.

The funny thing about Granddaddy Thomas is I remember very few words he ever said. I don't ever remember his having a conversation with me. I can't even remember the sound of his voice. But I remember his love. He showed his love to me every time I saw him in everything he did. He lived his love for me.

When we live our lives in a relationship with God, we live the love of our Heavenly Father and touch others for Him as we see, learn, feel and know His love for us. As we are enveloped in His love, we love others for Him and to Him. What a gift: to know we are loved and to love others into a relationship with our Heavenly Father. Our love for God and our love for others is expressed by word and by action.

Judy Williams

*This is the confidence we have in approaching God;
That, if we ask anything according to His will, He hears us.
And if we know that He hears us—whatever we ask—we know that
we have what we asked of Him.*

I John 5:14-15

CHAPTER SEVEN

Letters to Santa

A Christmas Story

*I*n my hometown everybody believed in Santa…at least that's how I remember Christmas as a child. At Christmastime there was a spirit of magic present; sugar plums really did dance in the air. There were contests in the town to see who had decorated their yard the best—and all the yards were beautiful. My favorite Christmas tree was always the one in the window of the Georgia Power and Light Company. I couldn't wait for that tree to be put up because that was a signal that Christmas was finally here! And that tree was decorated to the utmost with icicles, each one hanging straight down. There must have been a million icicles.

All the children in our town wrote letters to Santa. These letters were read over the local radio station each day of December before Christmas at 6:00 p.m. The letters usually followed a general format. The children began by stating how good they had been during the year: obeying their parents, listening to their teachers, saying prayers each night. This would be followed by asking Santa to please remember all the poor children, not only in our town but in the world, and to be sure each of these poor children had toys. At the end of the Christmas letter, each child listed the items they wanted, ranked in order of importance. The letter always closed by assuring Santa that cookies and milk would be left for him on the hearth.

My sister and I could not wait for our letter to be read over the radio. We would sit with anticipation listening to the letters from "all over the world." When our letter was finally read and our names called out at the end, we KNEW Santa had received our request. We jumped up and down and laughed and danced for joy! We had no doubt of receiving what we had requested.

I believe our prayers are like those letters to Santa. The moment we send them, our Heavenly Father receives and "reads" them. What joy, peace and anticipation should fill our hearts as we lay our requests before Him and know that He has not only "read" and heard them, but He will also fulfill them. He will answer our prayers.

I do believe that our Heavenly Father hears and immediately answers our prayers. However, sometimes "my" answers are not His answers. I often have tunnel vision after I have prayed and only see what I want the answer to my prayer to be.

In recent years I have learned to pray an additional sentence or two at the end of my "request time," asking my Heavenly Father to open my eyes to see what His answer is. I ask Him to expand my vision to see His will so that my prayer always and forever will be according to His will. And I ask Him to fill me with His peace as I wait and watch.

Judy Williams

If you... know how to give good gifts to your children,
how much more will your Father in heaven
give good gifts to those who ask him!

Matthew 7:11

CHAPTER EIGHT

To Be Forgiven

And The Peace That Comes After

When I was in high school Daddy bought our family a ski boat. It was a small boat, second-hand, and made of wood, but it was the most wonderful boat we had ever seen. Every weekend we would take the boat to Cherry Lake and water ski. Daddy would drive the boat and pull my sister and me and our friends around that lake for hours.

Daddy taught my sister and me how to drive the boat. And then he taught us how to pull the boat behind the car, and, an even more difficult task, how to back the car with the boat attached to it. These were the days when cars were large…there was no such thing as a compact car. Not only were the cars large, they had "fins" on the back, giving them a very square but almost "about to fly" look.

One day my sister and I were going to the lake with friends and of course we were taking the boat. We were so excited as we packed a picnic lunch, set times to pick up friends, gathered our suits and towels and headed for the car. I would be driving.

As I was pulling the car and boat out of the driveway, I had to do some maneuvering to get it straight, and it was necessary for me to back up a little. Whenever a boat trailer is attached to your car and you want to back up, you must turn the steering wheel in the opposite direction you want the car to go in order to make the attached vehicle turn in the correct direction.

In trying to back the car and boat that day, I forgot that lesson! As a result of this mistake, one of the "fins" punctured the wooden hull. I was devastated! I had ruined the boat. I could not face my daddy…I didn't want him to know what had happened. I didn't want him to know I had put a hole in our boat. How unreasonable was this thought? Of course he could see for himself the damage to the boat.

Over the next several days I avoided him.. I slept late in the mornings so he left for work before I awoke. I stayed out late in the evening with friends so he would be in bed before I came home. I don't know how long I thought I could continue avoiding him, but I was willing to postpone the inevitable confrontation for as long as I could.

One night he waited up for me. When I walked in the door, my heart sank. There he was sitting on the sofa determined to talk with me. He asked me to sit on the sofa beside him. Meekly and quietly I did so. His first words surprised me…they were not about the boat but were, "Judy, I am aware you have avoided me for the last few days. Why is that?" He was more concerned about my relationship with him than he was about the damage to the boat!

Tears poured out of my eyes and, with a trembling voice, I told him why I had been avoiding him, what I had done to the boat. Of course he already knew about the boat. That was not the question he wanted an answer to. He wanted to know why I had been avoiding him, not what I had done to the boat. I went on to explain how I had dreaded telling him because I was afraid he would be angry with me, or disappointed in me. I told him I just could not face telling him what I had done.

And then he said to me, "Judy, don't you know there is nothing, nothing in this world you could ever do that I would not forgive you for? Don't you know how much I love you?"

Wow! The power of love. The power of forgiveness. My father taught me a lesson about the love of God that day; about the forgiveness of God. My heavenly Father forgives me not only my unlovely thoughts, but also my unkind words and revengeful actions. He helps me learn to love as He does, by His forgiveness. What a wonderful earthly father. What a wonderful Heavenly Father.

Wives, submit to your husbands...
Husbands, love your wives...
Children, obey your parents.

Colossians 3:18ff

CHAPTER NINE

Yum!

Grannies Can Cook!

I have a big wooden dough bowl at my house and every time I look at it, I think of my Granny Thomas. I can still see her hands covered in flour as she cut in the Crisco shortening until the flour looked like fine meal. Then she made a little hole in the center into which she poured *real* milk. Gradually she pulled the Crisco mixed with flour into that little puddle of milk to make biscuit dough.

When the dough was just the right consistency, she would roll it out onto a floured cloth and cut the biscuits. Of course, around the edges there were always small scraps of dough and instead of rolling all those scraps into another biscuit, Granny would let me eat the dough. Yum! Raw biscuit dough!

In the fall when the apples were ripe, Granny would peel and cook those fresh apples until they were soft and oh so sweet. Then she would make her dough again and roll it out very thin, put a scoop of those stewed apples in the middle, fold the dough over the apples like an envelope and "ruffle" the edge, sealing the apples inside. The hot, melted Crisco grease was waiting as she dropped those apple fritters in and fried them until they were crispy and golden. My mouth waters to this day when I think about Granny's apple fritters.

I never remember eating Sunday dinner anywhere except at Granny's house. the menu was always the same: fried chicken (and sometimes the chicken had come straight from the back yard, caught, neck wrung, plucked and prepared the day before), mashed potatoes made with "real" milk and "real" butter, English peas which were always put on top of the mashed potatoes, and those homemade biscuits. Of course, sweet tea was the standard beverage.

As my whole family sat around that kitchen table every Sunday, we talked with each other. We shared the week's events. We planned for the days ahead. We laughed. Sunday, like no other day, was a day of family togetherness.

After lunch we all helped clean up. Since there was very little refrigerator space, all the leftover food was put in a pie safe that my Granddaddy Thomas had made years before. Before we left to go home in the late afternoon, those leftovers would be taken out of the pie safe and the whole delicious meal eaten again!

Family time. Love time. Sharing time. Good food and wonderful memories. I'll bet this is what Jesus experienced at the Last Supper. I'll bet His disciples cherished this moment, too.

Judy Williams

*Dear friends, let us love one another,
for love comes from God.
Everyone who loves has been born of God
and knows God.*

I John 4:7

CHAPTER TEN

While There Is Still Time

Ask The Questions...Learn The Answers

My Granny Thomas was old. The years had passed... where had those years gone? She was in her late 80s and living with my parents. Her mind had begun to "slip" a little bit. One day I began thinking about her homemade pumpkin pies. She made these pies every fall when the autumn leaves had begun to drift off the trees and "frost was on the pumpkin."

Her pumpkin pies were different from any other pumpkin pies I have ever tasted. She began, of course, with her homemade crust. Then, she mixed up the pie filling and baked it. That sounds like any other pumpkin pie, but what made her pies different were the spices she put in it. Her pies contained none of those "pumpkin" spices that give ordinary pumpkin pies a "twang." Her pies were made like custard, a pumpkin custard, with cream and eggs and butter and sugar, and vanilla. No strong pumpkin pie taste, just a pure pumpkin custard pie. She gave these pies to all her family and friends every fall.

Many years had passed since my childhood, and as I visited with Granny at my parents' home, I began to talk with her about my memories of her pumpkin pies. I talked about her making them and how delicious they were and how she made them every year and gave them to everyone she knew. Then I asked her, "Granny, can you give me your recipe for pumpkin pie?"

She replied to me, "Judy, I've never made a pumpkin pie in my life."

I had waited too long! The recipe was gone. Now I have only my memories, a poor substitute, to whet my appetite when I long for Granny's pumpkin pie.

There are so many things we need to talk about with our loved ones, so many questions we need to ask, so many amends to make while there is still time.

It's important to remember some of the experiences of our younger days. All experiences teach us something. And when we can combine memories with activities in the present — like making Granny's pumpkin pie — these memories are not only good for us but also for those loved ones who surround us, too. We can keep these memories alive and current not only by asking questions but by recording in words or pictures, making scrapbooks to pass along to our children and grandchildren.

Part II
THE AWAKENING

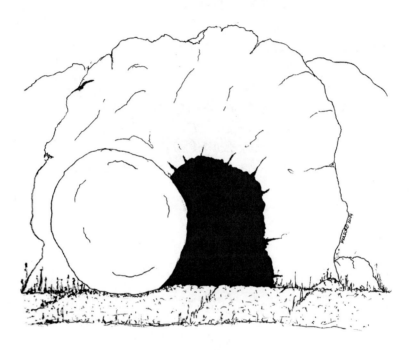

W hen I first turned to Jesus and opened the door of my heart for Him to come in, it was just a beginning. I stayed in this "beginning" phase of my Christian life for many years while Jesus waited for me to allow Him to be the Lord of my life. During these years He never ceased to be patient with me... nor did He cease to continue teaching me.

But the Counselor, the Holy Spirit,
whom the Father will send in my name,
will teach you all things
and will remind you of everything I have said to you.

John 14:26

CHAPTER ELEVEN

A New Life

Beginning To Walk The Path Of Light

*I*t wasn't until I was 16 or 17 years old that I turned to face God for the first time and He began His work of perfecting me, bringing me to completion. This was the period before television was in every home. In fact I only knew of one family who had a TV. It was a time before teenagers had their own cars. If we needed to go somewhere, we borrowed our parents' car. Our social life as teenagers consisted primarily of doing things with our church groups.

An evangelist came to town that summer and preached a revival in the brand new movie theater on the north side of Valdosta. The theater was packed every night. All my friends attended; practically everyone in the high school attended. Sometime during that week, the evangelist preached a sermon that touched my heart and it touched the hearts of most of my friends. At the end of the sermon, when the invitation came to make the decision to give my life to Christ, I walked down the aisle and said "Yes." Jesus made it easy for me to accept His invitation because many of my friends also committed their lives to Christ that evening.

My friends and I talked during the next few days about the decisions we had made, about how the evangelist had said to watch out because Satan would try to interrupt our lives since we now belonged to Jesus. I knew I belonged to Jesus. I had asked Him into my heart and He was there to stay. I began walking on the Path to Perfection—a very wide path at that time and one which included all my friends.

Over the next several years I did not do anything spectacular with my Christian faith. I was a good person, a moral person. I went to church every week, read my Bible sometimes, prayed sometimes, until I went off to college. Then I only went to church when I came home to visit. A few years passed, Jimmy and I met, and eventually married and had a family.

We went to church once in a while, and as our children got a little older we went to church a little more frequently. I probably read a devotional most days, but I was not consistent. Then, the alarm clock began to go off…God's alarm clock! I was 35 years old and for me it was a year of change!

The first alarm sounded in the spring when I had to have some very minor surgery, but I *knew* my life was in jeopardy. I was convinced the news following the surgery would be devastating and I would die. The surgery found nothing seriously wrong but the entire event made me look at myself differently. It made me question my faith…why had I been so afraid? I was a Christian, so what was the matter? Christians weren't supposed to be fearful.

The second alarm went off that summer. I was summoned for jury duty and it was my first experience with the legal system of our country. What an exciting adventure for me—a stay-at-home mom, who would for a few days get out of the house and even earn a little money. It was going to be a vacation. If I were "lucky," I might get put on a jury and have the whole week off!

I was the first to arrive at the Clarke County Courthouse that Monday morning. As the room began to fill, I was busy looking around to see who all was there and visiting with people I had not seen in a long time. The judge entered and everyone got quiet. He gave a few instructions and then he called my name—first name on the list. I stood as he asked me some questions. During the next few hours everyone in the courtroom answered most or all of those same questions.

After lunch, as we reconvened in the courtroom, the judge called my name right off the top of the list again. This time he told me to sit in the jury box. I then realized I was the first to be placed on a jury. When a second juror was seated I asked her what the case was. "It's a murder case," she said.

So began the worst "vacation" of my life. We found the young man guilty and he was sentenced to life in prison. In the following weeks I couldn't stop thinking about the trial and its results. I replayed the trial and deliberations over and over in my mind. I cried, talked to Jimmy, talked to friends, talked to my parents. The problem wasn't that the defendant wasn't guilty, because he was. The problem was that I didn't *want* the young man to be guilty. I didn't want him to go to jail for the rest of his life. Being the compassionate person that I am, I wanted to help him, give him another chance. I worried about his going to jail, what harm might come to him.

After a couple of weeks of this fretfulness and anxiety, a friend said to me, "Judy, you have worried about this so much and you can't get over it. Are you sure you are a Christian?" Once again I began to question my faith.

In the fall of that same year the third alarm made me get out of bed and seriously re-evaluate my life, my faith, my walk with Jesus. Our son Vince was ten years old and there was a lot of friction between the two of us. I couldn't communicate with him and he could not communicate with me. We were constantly at cross hairs. He always had to have the last word, but I also wanted the last word. I worried about him entering the pre-teen years and I could imagine all kinds of trouble ahead. Then one Sunday morning as our family was sitting together in church, Vince turned to me and said, "Mom, I want to give my life to Jesus today." And he walked down the aisle at the end of the service and asked Jesus to come into his heart.

I identify these three "awakenings" in my life that year as alarm clocks. They were touches or pushes from God for me to wake up and begin life anew. They were the awakening of an awareness of God in my life, and of a desire to have Him more fully involved in my life. It was a year of re-evaluation.

In our human life we will always have some anxiety, some worry and this does not mean we are not Christians. However, in this situation I knew I was not where I was supposed to be in my spiritual walk with Jesus. I opened my heart and began to allow the Spirit of God to come in. I began to pray every morning. Through Divine Intervention I was led to a Bible study group, and the leader of that group began to mentor me. For the next couple of years I studied under this wonderful Christian friend, and I began to allow the Holy Spirit of God, the Mind of Christ, to fill me and to teach me; to counsel me, comfort me, correct me, to remind me of all Jesus had said and taught me. I began to allow Jesus to become Lord and Savior of my life.

Judy Williams

For God so loved the world that
He gave His one and only Son,
that whoever believes in him
shall not perish but have eternal life.

John 3:16

CHAPTER TWELVE

Learning My Value

One Of The (Many) Hard Lessons

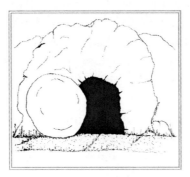

Jimmy's sister, Betty Carole, was a beautiful girl. In fact she had been a beauty queen in her high school and the Key Club Sweetheart, as well as holding many other awards. Betty was also very smart—salutatorian of her high school graduating class. Beautiful, intelligent, popular—everything a girl wants to be.

Some nineteen years after earning those awards, she hit the bottom. She was going through her second divorce and on several occasions, she had suffered from emotional problems which required hospitalization for several months each time. One particular time when she was discharged from the hospital, she had nowhere to go. Jimmy and I invited her into our home to stay until she could get on her feet.

We felt we could help her. In our growing faith we thought we had the answers, and we began our "ministry" with much enthusiasm. However, we learned that we all must make our own choices. As much as we wanted to help and as much as we tried to help her, Betty had to make her own life choices. The months passed and there were good days and bad days. The second year of her living with us came and went and life became very edgy in our home. Patience had reached its limit and the stress in every area of my life was taking its toll.

As we moved into the third year of Betty living with us, I knew I didn't want to be in this "ministry" any longer. Anger was growing in me; and bitterness, and resentment, and disappointment. I was envious of people who had normal families. Selfishness and indifference filled me. If you had known me during those years, you probably would not have thought anything was wrong in my life, but you would have been looking at the outside only. God was looking at my heart.

One day I began to see the real Judy. The self-centered, mean-spirited, indifferent, ugly Judy. I saw the human me. I saw the "me" from which my every action was motivated—an ugly me. And God in His very patient voice said to me, "And now, Judy, you know why I had to send my Son to die for you." It wasn't that I was doing anything bad or wrong or hurtful that anyone could see...the problem was *inside* me. I could not be the best I could be. I could not be what God wanted me to be as long as I allowed the "human" or "mammon" me to control me. I could not be the person God created me to be until I allowed the Presence of God to fill me and be the Motivator of my every action. In other words, I could not show the kindness of God, nor could I exhibit the forgiveness of God, nor could I express the love of God to others unless I allowed the Divinity of God to fill me.

Betty left our home after living with us almost three years. She became more independent, although she continued to have emotional problems and episodes of serious depression. On occasion she would need to be hospitalized. Jimmy and I always stood by her and supported her during her difficult times. My relationship with Betty was congenial, but we were never close.

Unless I am covered in the righteousness of Jesus, unless I am cleansed by His blood, I can never be what God wants me to be. Yes, now I did realize why Jesus had to die for me. No longer in my devotional time when I came to the part about confessing my sin would I sit and try to think of something I had done wrong so I could "confess" it. I now knew how unworthy I was to stand in the presence of God, except for the righteousness of my Savior.

Those same emotions, feelings, and ugliness still live in me. Envy, jealousy, resentment, anger, selfishness and indifference will still crop up in me at the most inopportune moments...without a hint of warning. I must claim Jesus' blood and righteousness every day because He loves me and I am His most prized possession. This is the way He wants each one of us to see ourselves. Because I am valuable to Him He has given me the security to look at my faults.

A short time later Betty Carole moved out of our home and moved on with her life. I look back on those years with great sadness. I wish I could have been a better example to her of the love of God. I grew closer to God through those days and I learned from Him about choices. I learned from Him my moment-by-moment need of Him.

Where can I go from your Spirit?
Where can I flee from your presence?
If I go up to the heavens, you are there;
if I make my bed in the depths,
you are there.

Psalm 139: 7,8

CHAPTER THIRTEEN

Ashley's Story

A Story Of The Presence Of God In Crisis

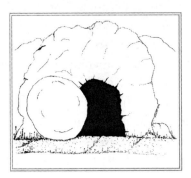

*I*t was the summer our daughter Ashley would turn 16. Summer vacation for her had just begun and we decided to go see the "hot" movie out—*Indiana Jones and the Last Crusade.* She had been complaining of headaches and feelings of pressure behind her eyes for a couple of weeks and I had taken her to the ophthalmologist who found nothing wrong.

I rushed home from work and picked her up. She grabbed a couple of aspirin to take since her headache was back and we ran by and picked up her Dad to go with us to the movie. We arrived to a packed theater and had to sit a few rows from the front in order to sit together.

At the climax of the film I noticed Ashley had slipped to the floor and was lying under the seats! She was (we later learned) having a grand mal seizure. At the hospital over the next couple of days, a diagnosis was made of aseptic meningitis. During the next two weeks, her headaches became worse, her fever would reach peaks in excess of 103 at times. Her bladder function stopped and the urologist told us the meningitis virus often attacks the bladder.

Ashley was sent home from the hospital after two weeks. Her fever continued to go up each day, the headaches became more intense. Because of her bladder problem she had to catheterize herself every four hours. Another two weeks passed and the headaches were not so intense, the fevers not quite so high and her bladder function began to improve. However, as all of these symptoms began improving, she began to experience other strange symptoms: she began to lose her balance, eventually not being able to walk without someone holding her; her eyes began "jumping" and not in synchrony with each other; she complained of a roaring in her ears as though they were filled with water.

We took her back to the neurologist who immediately hospitalized her once again. Tests showed that Ashley was having severe neurological problems, and she was transferred by ambulance to Emory University Hospital in Atlanta where she was admitted to ICU.

At Emory her situation went from bad to worse. At her lowest point Ashley could no longer recognize her sister. She had no concept of what day/week/year it was. She could not carry on a conversation. Ashley had lost the ability to control her bowel or bladder, and she would go into deep sleep from which she would have to be shaken and yelled at to awaken. She was completely blind in her right eye and had lost 90% of the vision in her left eye.

On Friday morning, the end of her first week at Emory, she was being taken to the hearing clinic for tests. She was tied in the wheelchair so she would not fall out since she could no longer sit up by herself. She looked like a little rag doll. The hearing test was made and she and I awaited the results. The doctor told us she was completely deaf in her left ear and had lost 90% of her hearing in her right ear. We sat and waited for the attendant to come and transport her back to her room.

As I watched Ashley, a million questions and worries filled my mind: Would she ever see again, hear again? Would she walk, speak, or ever recognize any of us? Would she live, die, or ever leave the hospital? What if they discharged her in this condition? What would we do? As I watched her, thinking, pondering, worrying and afraid, she began to lift her head. She sat up a little straighter, and she then began to sing in a very clear voice:

> *God is so good; God is so good,*
> *God is so good, He's so good to me.*
> *God answers prayer, God answers prayer,*
> *God answers prayer, He's so good to me.*
> *I love Him so, I love Him so,*
> *I love Him so, He's so good to me.*

Then, Ashley once again dropped her head and folded back into her non-responsive, rag doll, position.

God spoke to me in that moment. He said, "I'm here. I promised you I would never leave you or forsake you, and I'm here. I am walking with you through this Valley of the Shadow of Death. You are not alone." My God did not tell me Ashley would be all right. He did not tell me she would be healed. He did not tell me she would live. My God simply told me that He was present…I was not alone sitting beside my critically ill child. He reminded me of His love, and His care, and His concern. He told me there is nowhere I can go—to the heights of Heaven or the depths of Hell—that He is not there awaiting me.

When we returned to Ashley's hospital room, I called Ashley's father, who had gone back to our home in Athens the evening before. I told him he needed to return to Emory immediately. I told him that Ashley was dying. Every bodily function in her system was shutting down. When Jimmy arrived he, Ashley's sister, Tracy, and I laid our hands on Ashley and prayed for her. We asked God to intervene and heal her with His Master Physician's touch. Then we placed her in the arms of Jesus for God's will to be accomplished.

Around 8:00 p.m. Ashley's team of doctors came into her room. They told us they believed the meningitis virus had attacked Ashley's brain stem because it was completely inflamed. They would begin treating her with high doses of steroids immediately. (Until this point only antibiotics had been used to treat Ashley.)

Saturday morning we could see a very, very slight improvement. Each day Ashley improved a little more. At the end of her second week at Emory she was discharged. Two weeks later she began her sophomore year of high school with her classmates. Within a year she was completely healed.

God had plans for Ashley, plans for good and not for evil; plans which gave her a future and a hope. God has plans for each one of us. He wants each one of us to be saved and to come to the knowledge of the truth; then He wants each one of us to go into this hurting world and spread the good news of His hope.

Judy Williams

Before they call I will answer,
While they are still speaking I will hear.

Isaiah 65:24

CHAPTER FOURTEEN

Traci's Ring

A Treasure Lost And Found

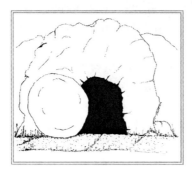

*I*t was the Christmas season. I was shopping with my daughter-in-law Traci and my granddaughter Marie. We had visited every store in Columbia. I was worn out, but they, in their youth, were still going strong. We were to meet Vince, our son, and the rest of the family at a local restaurant for dinner.

"One more store," Traci and Marie said to me, and it was a big one, similar to a World Bazaar with everything imaginable in it. We walked in and turned to the right where there were aisle after aisle of bins containing small toys, knick knacks, stuffed animals and the like reaching almost to the ceiling. Traci and Marie stopped here and I continued on through the store.

I was amazed at all the items in this store, and it took me a while to go through it. I began making my way back to the place I had last seen my fellow-shoppers. After an hour of "shopping," I certainly did not expect to find them in the same place I had left them…but there they were. However, their faces were not those of happy shoppers and I knew immediately something had happened.

Just after we had separated earlier Marie had jokingly picked up a small, stuffed toy snake. After telling her mother to "Think fast!" she threw the "snake" at Traci. Traci, unfortunately at that moment, was fiddling with her ring given to her by Vince on their 10th wedding anniversary and she jumped as she saw the snake flying at her. Her anniversary ring flew, landing in one of the many bins. While I had been wandering through the store, they had been searching through thousands of items in as many bins as they could reach.

Traci's eyes were filling with tears as she related the facts to me. I said to her, "Traci, we're going to find that ring," and I began to search. They stood and watched me now searching with the frenzy they had been searching for the past hour. The more I searched the more I knew we must pray, but I didn't know how they would receive this suggestion—praying in the middle of a busy store filled with holiday shoppers. So, I looked up at Traci and said to her, "Traci, how do you feel about praying?"

"I'm all for it," she replied.

I pulled Traci and Marie down to their knees with me and we prayed to the God who knows everything. We prayed to the God in whose eyes nothing is lost. We thanked Him for the years of love and marriage which the gift of the ring represented for this family which was under His guidance. We thanked Him for the opportunity to pray, in this store, among the crowds of people, for an item which He knew meant so much more to Traci than just a ring. We asked Him to tell us where to search since He knew exactly where the ring was; and we thanked Him for hearing our request and for answering even before we asked.

Then each of us reached into a bin. "Oh my God," Traci said as she pulled out her ring on the very first search of a bin she had already looked through several times before.

"Exactly," I said, "Oh my God." Praise God from Whom all blessings flow.

A little later Traci asked me, "Judy, do you always have your prayers answered that quickly?" What a thought-provoking question.

"Yes," I told her, "He always answers me 'before I call'."

Our Heavenly Father knows what we need before we ask. However, many times I don't recognize His answer because I am so focused on what I think the answer should be. So my first prayer request most often is, "Lord, not only may I pray according to Your will, but may I recognize your answer."

As a man thinks within himself,
so he is.

Proverbs 23:7a NASB

CHAPTER FIFTEEN

Unexpected Feelings

The Ugly Ones Never Go Away

When my sister and I were little, our parents put us in "Expression" classes. Through a number of these classes over the years, we learned how to perform in public by readings, dancing, being in plays, etc. One year when we were about 10 years old, we were going to have minor parts in a play. I can't tell you the name of the play or anything about it except the parts Julie and I were assigned.

She, my twin sister, got the part of Flash, the Bright Star. Her costume was so cute. She got to wear little black net stockings, a little black leotard with a cape attached, all of which sparkled with rhinestones, as well as a little black skull cap which had glitter all over it. And she got to wear rouge and lots of beautiful makeup. Flash, the Bright Star.

I was cast in the part of Brunhilda, the maid. My costume consisted of dowdy clothes, a dust scarf on my head, lace-up shoes with stretched-out socks falling down around my ankles. Can you imagine what my feelings were when I compared my sister and her costume to me and my costume? Anger, jealousy, bitterness, resentment. This was my first lesson in how unfair life could be.

That's the thing about feelings: we can't do anything about them. They just come up in us. Sometimes—most of the time—they come up without any warning. Our feelings are part of what makes us who we are. We can't do anything about our feelings, but we can do something about the way we react to our feelings.

I never told Julie or my parents or anyone else how I felt about the differences in our costumes. I held my feelings in. After the play had finished its run, I don't remember ever thinking again about how I felt in those days until I wrote this story. Experiences like this one help to make us the people we become as adults. We can choose to learn from these difficult experiences to make better decisions. When I am hurt or upset now, I try to address the problem immediately and not hold my feelings in.

Philippians 4:8 tells us to keep our minds focused on the things that are true, noble, right, pure, lovely, admirable, excellent, praiseworthy – things that are of God. And the God of peace will be with us (my paraphrase). When we turn our thoughts and minds to the goodness of God in the midst of our tumultuous feelings, we can be sure His peace will fill us.

Judy Williams

This day I call heaven and earth as witnesses against you
that I have set before you life and death, blessings and curses.
Now choose life, so that you and your children may live,
and that you may love the Lord your God,
listen to His voice, and hold fast to Him.
For the Lord is your life,
and He will give you many years in the land
He swore to give to your fathers, Abraham, Isaac and Jacob.

Deuteronomy 30:19-20

CHAPTER SIXTEEN

Our Greatest Freedom

A Formula For Life

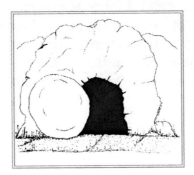

The greatest freedom we have is the freedom to choose: so, choose wisely. The freedom to choose is truly a gift from God. I used to read the poem "Invictus" by William Ernest Henley—and particularly the last verse—with such sadness, feeling that the poet did not know God:

> It matters not how strait the gate
> How charged with punishment the scroll,
> I am the master of my fate;
> I am the captain of my soul.

Now I look at the poem differently. We are truly the "masters of our fates; the captains of our souls" because God has given us the gift of choice. All of us are the sum product of the choices we have made. We cannot say "So-and-so made me do it," or "I am a product of my environment," or "If only I had had different/more attentive/more loving/understanding parents or spouse." We all choose how we will act or react in any and every situation. As we get older the gift of choice becomes even more important because then we have the opportunity to change some of our bad choices into good ones.

Our God has given us the gift of choosing life or death, the gift of choosing to follow Him or deny Him. Moses, in his final sermon to the people of Israel, urged them to "Choose life, so that you and your children may live, and that you may love the Lord your God, listen to His voice, and hold fast to Him. For the Lord is your life." (Deuteronomy 30:19)
This day choose life!

Judy Williams

Cleanse me with hyssop, and I will be clean;
wash me, and I will be whiter than snow.

Psalm 51:7

CHAPTER SEVENTEEN

The White Vest

Why We Need A Savior

*B*efore my husband retired we were invited to his boss's annual Christmas dinner party hosted by him and his wife at their beautiful home. This party was always a very elegant and exclusive affair as some of the most prominent men and women in the company for which Jimmy worked attended. I always took special care about what I wore because I wanted to look my very best. I also tried to stay near Jimmy because he knew all these people and to me they were basically strangers whom I saw once a year. This particular evening I was wearing a white wool vest as part of my Christmas attire.

Soon after we arrived we were served glasses of red wine. I was standing in the hallway talking with a couple of the wives when someone accidently made a gesture which knocked my elbow. Red wine spilled down my white vest and onto the white carpet of the hallway.

Mortified, I immediately knelt and began trying to dab the red stain up with my little cocktail napkin. The lady who knocked my elbow left. Jimmy was nowhere to be seen. I was now in the hallway alone where only moments before a crowd had been standing. I knew everyone was distancing themselves from the disaster on the white carpet.

Within a few moments I noticed someone kneeling beside me, dabbing the stain with her cocktail napkin. It was the boss's wife. "I am so sorry," I said to her.

"Don't worry, Judy. We were going to replace this carpet anyway," she replied. Her statement did not make me feel any better.

Then she stood up, rushed into her laundry room and brought out a spray bottle.. She sprayed the damaged carpet. The red wine color began to fade. She sprayed the carpet again and the stain completely disappeared. Unbelievingly, I watched the red wine stain disappear with my own eyes.

"What is in the bottle?" I asked her.

"It's OxiClean," she said. "When I bought it the salesman told me it would take stains out of anything. I'm glad I remembered it."

Amazed, I asked her if she would spray my white wool vest. She did, and the red wine stain disappeared completely from my vest.

I still have that vest. I wear it every year at Christmas. The stain has never come back. It is as if I had never spilled the wine.

Removing the stain from the carpet and my vest reminded me how the blood of Jesus removes the stain of sin from my heart. His blood completely washes me clean. No amount of OxiClean, is ever going to cleanse the hardness of my heart, where my sin begins. Sometimes I may try outward "cleansers" such as good works, reading/teaching the Bible, or giving extra money to the church to help me "feel" better or, to the outside world, look better. But, my good actions done specifically for these reasons only clean the outside of me. Like OxiClean, good works done only to make me look or feel better only cover up the stain and help to cover the consequences of my sin. Only the blood of Jesus, the Lamb of Calvary can cleanse me from the inside and make me whole, make me new.

Judy Williams

Part III
SPIRITUAL GROWTH

I have learned to watch for God every day in every way. I am constantly surprised by the very unexpected ways He reveals Himself and His very great love for me. It may take me a day or two or even longer to realize what He has said to me and what He wants me to learn, but He knows what a poor student I can sometimes be.

Whatever happens,
conduct yourselves in a manner worthy of the gospel of Christ.

Philippians 1:27a

CHAPTER EIGHTEEN

The Friend Who Watched

Our Lives Are The Only Bible Some People Read

*O*ne day a friend came to visit and have a cup of tea. We do this sometimes, this friend and I, and we share what's going on in our lives with each other. On this particular day, life seemed to be laying a little heavy on my friend's heart. After we had talked a little while about the deep hole she found herself in, she said to me, "Judy, I've watched you and Jimmy over the many years we have known each other and you have both been through some pretty tough times. I don't know how you got through some of them.

"As I have watched you and Jimmy in these difficult circumstances, you have both come through them with such a calmness about you. You have braved hard times much better than some of my other friends. How did you do it? How did you get through those times without having trouble in your marriage?"

Jimmy and I have been through tough times—a critically ill child, broken relationships, sick relatives living with us for extended periods of time. Some days were so difficult I questioned my faith in God. During those days Jimmy and I turned to God. We prayed. We talked with each other, always keeping the lines of communication open. We worshipped regularly and read our Bibles seeking God's wisdom and God's guidance.

As Jimmy and I made it through each difficult period, we grew in our spiritual walk. We grew in our faith. We began to realize how much we learn as we walk in the valleys and how much our difficult times enable us to appreciate the mountain tops.

I was talking with a friend recently and he was recounting to me some days of hardship in his family. He said there was a period of time when he and his wife were considering, and even discussing divorce. This couple stuck it out through those trying times and now, some twenty years later as they celebrate and enjoy their children and grandchildren, they are so glad they did. This man said to me that day when he was remembering the hard times, "Judy, I'm so glad we made it through 'those' days to get to 'these' days, because 'these' days are the best days of our lives." This man, his wife and their family learned to depend on God.

This particular morning as I sat having tea with my friend, I was able to share with her my love of God. I was able to share with her how much God loves each one of us; cares for us. I was able to share with her that despite walking through tough times – times which could bring destruction to a marriage – Jimmy and I were united in our love of Jesus, and through Him, we were united in our love and respect for one another. The times were tough, I will admit, but walking in those valleys Jimmy and I learned more of God, more of God's love for us, and how to more deeply love each other and others.

We never know who may be watching us, listening to us, reading God's Word in us.

Judy Williams

I confess my iniquity;
I am troubled by my sin.

Psalm 38:18

CHAPTER NINETEEN

I'm Sorry

At Times We All Need To Say "I'm Sorry"

*I*t was Christmas Eve, 2007. We were waiting in the narthex of our church for our daughter Ashley and her family to join us for the Christmas Eve "family" Service—the one geared toward families with young children.

Finally, in the door they came, Logan running up to me, and nearly knocking me down with his exuberant hug, and Hunter grabbing his Papa with his arms. They were so excited that Christmas was here and their joy was spilling over into their words and actions.

Logan and Hunter went into the sanctuary and sat down in one of the pews. We adults followed a few minutes later. I don't know what happened between the narthex and the sanctuary, but by the time we reached the pew, Logan's mood had hit rock bottom. Throughout the service he was unruly, obstinate and disruptive and unresponsive to instructions and directions from his mother or me.

When we left the service, I whispered to him in the narthex, "Your actions in church tonight embarrassed me." I worried about him all the way home and throughout the evening. I talked to God about my concern but felt no peace even as we left the next morning to go to their house for Christmas celebration.

Logan's "big" toy was a drum set; and Hunter received a video game. They both wanted to show me these gifts. After a demonstration of each, Logan and I were sitting on the sofa watching Hunter play his new game when Logan quietly turned to look at me and said, "Grammy, I'm sorry about the way I acted in church last night. And, I apologized to Mama when I got home."

Oh, to be like a little child. Their hearts are so open to the love of God, and they are always so ready to make things "right." I thanked Logan and told him how proud I was of him, and yes, I forgave him. That night I prayed that I might be as this child in recognizing my wrongs and being willing to make them right, that I might be as willing as Logan to confess my sin and ask for the forgiveness of those whom I have hurt.

Judy Williams

Be still and know that I am God.

Psalm 46:10

CHAPTER TWENTY

Old Dog...New Tricks

We're Never Too Old To Learn

Old Dog was king of the house. He had outlasted all the "young uns" over the years. He slept where he wanted, ate when and where he wanted, and lazed under the shade of the trees on the rare occasions he asked to be let out of the house. Then... Jack arrived.

Pure mutt! No respect for his elders. No previous training about how to keep a clean house either...obviously...sloppy when eating, and trying to get some of Old Dog's food to boot. No manners whatsoever. Well, Old Dog would have to teach him. As the weeks passed, Old Dog realized this task was going to be more difficult than he had thought. Was he up to it?

Christmas came with all the confusion of a house with three children, four cats and two dogs. Well, scratch that. Old Dog didn't really consider himself in the same category with Jack. Two days after Christmas the presents had been opened, some already broken, most of the relatives had gone home and things were settling back down to normal.

Old Dog was lying in front of the fire on his favorite rug dreaming of days gone by. Suddenly his dreams were awakened by "quack, quack." Jack was playing with the toy he had received for Christmas—a stuffed duck that quacked when you squeezed it. His nap interrupted, Old Dog got up to move to a quieter, more private resting place. Jack followed with his toy. "Quack, quack."

Old Dog began to hurry along trying not to show his annoyance. Jack was right behind him. "Quack, quack." Old Dog began to run around and around the room. Jack was on his heels. "Quack, quack." Faster and faster went Old Dog around the sofa, around the chair, around the sofa, around the chair. "Quack, quack. Quack, quack. Quack, quack."

Just before he turned to butter, Old Dog gave up his escape and lay down exhausted. Jack put his head down in Old Dog's lap. "Quack, quack." Old Dog closed his eyes and rested.

When troubles come…when troubles rush at us, piling up 'til we think we can stand no more…when the noise of the day and the fears of the future fill our heads and our hearts and we can run, walk, sit, do no more: It's time to let go and let God be God. It's time to cease striving and know that the God of the universe is the God we worship and He loves each one of us. It's time to close our eyes and rest in Him.

Judy Williams

*We do not know what we ought to pray for,
but the Spirit himself intercedes for us
with groans that words cannot express.*

Romans 8:26b

CHAPTER TWENTY ONE

The Helper

The REAL Coast Guard

My daughter-in-law Traci and I decided to take her children to the Jeremy Cay Inlet at the end of the Edisto State Park beach to ride the creek as it went down to low tide and into the ocean. This is a very isolated beach we had visited earlier in the week with several of the children, but our grandson Chris had not been with us and we all decided it would be another fun day which would include him.

The tide was not as low as it had been previously, and the children did not get in the creek right away. When they asked "how long" before they could ride the current, I told them it would probably be 1½ to 2 hours before the creek would be at the level it was earlier in the week. They waited a little over an hour before they jumped in with their Boogie Boards to ride the creek's current as it entered the sea.

Eleven year old Gavin was the first down the creek. As soon as he stood up in the knee-deep water where it reached the sea, he realized he was in trouble and began calling for help. When someone is in knee-deep water, you can't believe they are in too much trouble, but Gavin continued to scream for help. His mother Traci and his older siblings Marie and Chris jumped in and went right to Gavin. I was standing on shore about fifteen feet away, watching.

Within seconds it was obvious that all of them, mom and three children, were in difficulty as they were swept 50 yards out into the ocean and beyond. Before I could blink an eye they were 75 yards out. Seeing they had only one small Boogie Board for the four of them to hold onto, I grabbed an inner tube and headed for the water. A man standing nearby on the beach, the only other person on the beach, mentioned calling 911, and I yelled to him where to find my cell phone.

As I rushed into the water two thoughts ran through my head: 1) with five of us in the grip of what I now realized was a rip current, we would probably not all (maybe not any) make it back safely; and 2) I was watching my son's entire family being swept out to sea and there was no way I could stand on the beach and do nothing.

I jumped in, praying that I would not only be able to get to my family who were in trouble, but also that I would not be swept too far to the right or left and out of their reach. The flotation device I was "dragging" would be large enough to put Gavin on while the rest of us could hold on to it. When Chris saw me coming out with a float, he decided he would try to break out of the rip current and swim back to the beach. He remembered exactly what to do: swim parallel to the beach, then turn toward shore. I passed him on my way out and he mentioned to me how exhausted he was, but he was almost at the water's edge.

The current took me straight to Traci. With her first words she also expressed how exhausted she was, but she was able to grab onto my float. Marie and Gavin, however, were not able to catch it. We were immediately separated into two groups. As hard as Traci and I tried we could not get back to Marie and Gavin.

When Marie realized she couldn't grab my float, with Gavin on the Boogie Board, she began pulling him and swimming parallel to the beach (we were all now over 100 yards out). She, too, remembered exactly what to do to escape a rip current. She kept her head and never panicked.

Traci and I were not so lucky. The harder we tried to reunite with the children, the farther out we were swept. I believe Traci and I were deeper in the midst of the current than any of the children and that's why we continued to be swept out to sea. At our farthest point the man on the beach estimated we were over 300 yards out. We continued to watch Marie and Gavin (two little "dots" in the water between swells now hundreds of yards away from us), but they looked like they were doing all right. At least they were not being swept out further as Traci and I were, and they were continuing to make progress toward the beach.

Traci and I continued trying to swim toward the children but could make no headway. We finally decided we needed to go in the opposite direction and away from the children to get out of the current. We could see small waves in that direction which meant the current was not there. This was a very hard decision to make as we continued to watch Marie and Gavin still in the water but very, very far away from us. At this time Traci and I both finally managed to get the upper part of our bodies onto the tube. Contrary to my earlier thoughts that this day would probably end in tragedy, I now felt with certainty that we would ALL make it to safety. I didn't understand how I could feel this way, being more than 300 yards out in the ocean; not to mention the fact that two children were still in the water and trying to make it to shore. I expressed this feeling to Traci and continued to tell her Marie and Gavin were going to be fine; they were doing well as they continued to swim toward shore. This was definitely God's peace filling me, because the circumstances themselves did not indicate that result.

Traci and I prayed. We asked the Lord to enclose Marie and Gavin in His arms of protection; to give them wisdom to know exactly what to do; to give them courage and peace in the face of fear and His strength to make it safely to shore.

In a short while we saw two more "match sticks" (which is about how large people appeared from our vantage point) on the beach, and could count all the children and one man now on the beach. Praise God.

We prayed for ourselves. We prayed that God would fill us with His wisdom to know exactly what we needed to do; that He would also be our strength and courage. And as we finally got on the far side of the rip currant, a wave slapped us gently on the back and gave us a definite "shove" in the direction of shore. "Thank you, Jesus," I said, "for the reminder that 'You are with us always, and You will never leave us or forsake us' (especially in our time of need)!" We still had a long way to go.

Traci and I kicked and paddled, and the shore got closer. Before long we could stand on the sandy bottom of the ocean and finally were able to walk in to shore. The children all crossed the inlet (much farther up) and ran to us. We enclosed each other with hugs of joy…and tears!

Water is a powerful force. I have seen its power on many occasions. But neither water nor any other power on earth compares with the power of God; the power of his love, his truth, his understanding, his mercy, his forgiveness, his faithfulness. Thank you, Jesus. That unforgettable day the Holy Spirit prayed for Traci and me. In our busyness, our fright, our lack of knowledge of what to do, The Holy Spirit prayed for us, and God heard.

Judy Williams

95

> *See, I have engraved you*
> *on the palms of my hands...*
>
> **Isaiah 49:16**

CHAPTER TWENTY TWO

Knowing Who You Are

Importance Is Relative

Julie is my identical twin. Growing up, Julie and I did everything together. We not only looked alike but we dressed alike, went everywhere together, and even had the same friends. We were also late bloomers. Very late bloomers. We didn't think we would ever grow out of our skinny, freckled faces and mousy brown hair immaturity. Finally, late in our junior year, we began to date a little. In fact, at that time I got my first boyfriend. Johnny and I had a few dates, then he asked me to "go steady" (that's what it was called back then). Johnny was not only really cute, he was also popular and very outgoing. I couldn't believe how lucky I was.

You know how you always remember your first boyfriend or girlfriend? The one who first reached over and held your hand as you were walking down the school hallway (my heart almost pounded out of my chest); the one who gave you your first "real" kiss. Your first boyfriend was important in your life. You became a little more self-assured – somebody besides your parents loved you. You got to go places, meet different people. You "belonged." Since Johnny was a senior that year, he was invited to lots of graduation parties both in his honor and in honor of his friends, and I got to go with him. Wow. Did I feel like I had "arrived!"

Many years passed and on rare occasions I would run into Johnny when I visited my home town. We'd chat a little, talk about our kids, our families, but that was the extent of our conversations for a very long time. However, a few years ago Julie and I were in Valdosta tying up some legal issues following the deaths of our parents when we ran into Johnny and had time for a real conversation.

Johnny and Julie and I all reminisced about our high school days and caught up on what had happened in our lives in the intervening years. We talked about the people we had known and past events, plans for the future. The visit was wonderful and we all hated for it to come to an end. However Johnny had to get back to work and Julie and I had many more things to attend to. Johnny got up to leave and as he reached the door he turned around, looked at Julie and me and said, "Now, which one of y'all did I date? Was it Judy or Julie?"

Wow. Someone who had been so important in my life, someone who had helped me "break out" of childhood into young adulthood, someone who gave me my first kiss, was the first love of my heart, didn't remember it was ME he dated! I couldn't believe it.

How fortunate we are to have Someone in our lives who will never get us mixed up with someone else, Someone who not only remembers every part of our lives, but considers those parts that we consider important to be very important to Him also. How fortunate we are to have Someone who has our names engraved on the palm of His hands, beside the scars on His hands; Someone who will never forget us: our Lord and Savior Jesus Christ.

Judy Williams

Now we see but a poor reflection as in a mirror

I Corinthians 13:12a

CHAPTER TWENTY THREE

The Watch

Dream On!

My watch had broken. It was not an expensive one since I have a history of being hard on watches, but now I needed a new one. It was quiet in the office that morning, so I told my co-worker, Lisa, I was going to run to Walmart and pick up a new watch. I intended to get one of those $12.95 watches.

As I walked toward the back of the jewelry department, a display table caught my eye. This table was covered in Disney watches: Mickey Mouse, Minnie Mouse, Donald Duck, Pluto, and all the other Disney characters we love so well. I stopped to look at these watches and thought, "Maybe I could spend just a little bit more..." Then, my eyes zoomed in on it—THE watch. The face was Cinderella, dressed in a silver gown with a sparkling tiara on her head. "Yes," I thought. "I could 'be' Cinderella." No second looks at any other watches...this was the one for me.

I went straight to the counter and paid for it. When I got to the car I took the watch out of all the packaging and put it on. I couldn't wait to show Lisa my Cinderella watch. I went straight to her desk when I got to the office, holding out my wrist for her to see.

"Oh, I like it, Judy. Eeyore has always been one of my favorite Disney characters."

EEYORE?! I snatched my wrist back, went to my desk and pulled out my reading glasses to look at my new watch more closely. There on the face of the watch was not Cinderella smiling at me but Eeyore grinning. Next time I go to buy a watch I WILL most definitely take my glasses with me.

Not seeing clearly the image on the face of the watch I was purchasing helped me to realize how limited my vision of God is through my human eyes. In this life I do not see God clearly -- the things of God, the love of God, the hopes/dreams/visions of God. My vision is impaired by my humanity with its sinfulness, self-centeredness, history, hurts and all the other parts of my life that make up me. I worship and love a God whose hopes and dreams, whose will and purpose, whose love and forgiveness are beyond anything I can imagine. Now I only see in part, know in part. But one day I shall know fully even as I am fully known.

Part IV

THE PATH BECOMES NARROW

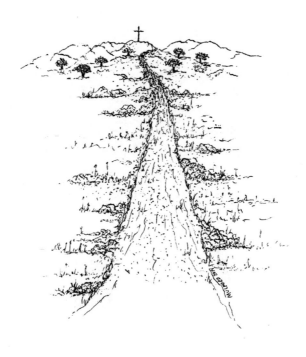

We have often heard that we should walk the straight and narrow path. When I began my journey of faith, my path was very wide. It included all my friends, all my family, basically everyone I knew. I would consult with these loved ones about where to walk, how fast to go, should I do "this or that" along the way. As I have grown in my spiritual life and grown in my awareness of my Savior in my life, my path has become narrow and He is the one whom I consult. He is the one who lights my way. My path is now only wide enough for the two of us.

Do not withhold good from those who deserve it,
when it is in your power to act.
Do not say to your neighbor,
'come back later; I'll give it tomorrow.'
when you now have it with you.

Proverbs 4:27,28

CHAPTER TWENTY FOUR

Expressing Love

It's Important To Say, "Well Done!"

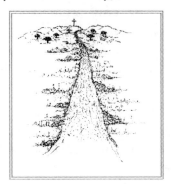

Recently I attended a wedding shower for a good friend's daughter. This party was a different kind of wedding shower because the couple—first marriage for both—requested no gifts. Instead they asked guests to bring their favorite pictures or photographs and share them because the wedding couple both love photography.

I had visited with the couple earlier in the week, and at that time, I told them I was going to bring a wedding picture of my grandparents and tell a story about them, a story about love in a marriage. At the shower, however, I knew very few people. I decided right away that I would not tell my story. I would just pass the picture of my grandparents around.

However, as the party got underway and people were passing around their pictures ("This was a picture we made when…" "Here is a picture of our children when they were little…" "We just liked this picture and wanted to bring it…") we all commented on how beautiful or unique each picture was. I decided I would show the picture of my grandparents and tell my story. When I finished, no one said a word. It was kind of an awkward moment…complete silence, people just looking at me. Since Jimmy and I had another engagement that evening, we left a short time later.

Two days later the mother of the bride called me and said, "Judy, I just wanted to call and thank you for telling your story about your grandparents. After you left, everyone began talking about it. One of the men came up to me and said that it really signified what the celebration of this upcoming marriage is about. This man said the story meant so very, very much to him." The story expressed the love of a husband and a wife for each other.

You know what I thanked my friend for? I thanked her for calling me…calling to relate those affirming comments. Many times I am quick to believe that silence after I have shared means disapproval. I am one of those people who needs audible words of confirmation.

Sometimes God uses us to speak a blessing to others. We may never know that this blessing has happened. When words of praise or affirmation are called for, we should always express them.

Judy Williams

If we are faithless, He will remain faithful;
for He cannot disown Himself.

II Timothy 2:1

CHAPTER TWENTY FIVE

Even if We Are Faithless, He Will Remain Faithful

Our Wonderful, Loving Heavenly Father

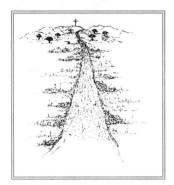

Have you ever felt faithless? Has there ever been a time when you just couldn't pull it in and pray because your faith was at the bottom of the bucket?

One night I went to sleep and it was one of those black, pitch dark nights when there was not a light in the sky. Several hours later I awoke to the brightest light filling my sunroom, which is next to my bedroom. The sunroom was so bright it appeared a light had been turned on. I walked out to look up in the sky and there was one of the fullest, brightest moons I had ever seen.

I realized the moon had been there in the sky all along, just where it always is...just where it is supposed to be. I had not been able to see the light because I was not in the right place. I went to bed faithless (in the dark), and when I awoke I realized the Light had been there with me all along.

Even in those moments when we are faithless, when we feel we can't go on, when we feel we are all alone, Our Heavenly Father remains faithful. He is right where we can always reach Him, talk to Him, be comforted by Him. He is right where we know He will always be, in our hearts, loving us. He has promised He will never leave us or forsake us and He keeps His promises.

Judy Williams

We are standing on Holy Ground,
And I know that there are angels all around.
Let us praise Jesus now,
We are standing in His Presence on Holy Ground.

From "Standing on Holy Ground"
lyrics by Geron Davis

CHAPTER TWENTY SIX

On Holy Ground
Standing In His Presence

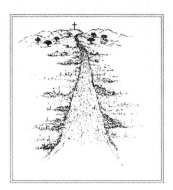

Jimmy and I attended a funeral some time ago where several members of a young family had been tragically killed in an automobile accident. In cases like these there is always a tremendous response by the people of the community in support of the family. This occasion was no exception. Many, many friends and relatives and co-workers attended the visitation and the funeral in love and support of the devastated surviving family members.

As I sat with one of the relatives of the family, I put my arm around her and I said, "Do you know Jesus is in this room?"

"Really?" she said...she questioned...she hoped.

"Yes," I replied.

"Do you feel this arm around your shoulders? It is the arm of Jesus. Have you heard words of comfort and love from these many friends and family who are here tonight? Their words come straight from the mouth of Jesus. Have you seen tears on the faces of your friends? Those are the tears of God. He is weeping with you. The man who brought you a cool glass of water a moment ago—Jesus is sustaining you. Jesus is everywhere you look in this room. Jesus is here."

When people allow us into their most intimate places, the place of their pain, the place of their fear, the place of their deepest concerns, they have allowed us into a Holy Place, a place where God resides. When we are obedient to God and walk with others through their pain, they will see Jesus in us. And we will see Jesus in them. "I tell you the truth, whatever you did for one of the least of these brothers of mine you did for me." (Matthew 25:40)

Judy Williams

You hem me in – behind and before;
You have laid your hand upon me.

Psalm 139: 5

CHAPTER TWENTY SEVEN

A Rude Awakening

When Life Hits Us In The Face

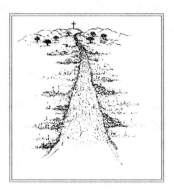

After the news services reported that a pack of wild dogs had killed someone in our county, I bought a small pepper spray to carry with me when I walk our country road alone. One morning I had put the pepper canister on the kitchen table intending to pick it up on my way out, but had been briefly distracted by an errand in the back of the house.

Jimmy sat down to eat his bowl of cereal at the kitchen table. He noticed the small black canister and, thinking it was a small flashlight, picked it up to see if the "light" was working (don't we all do that when we pick up a flashlight?) He pointed the "light" at his face, pressed the button to turn it on and got the full load of pepper spray in his face.

I heard the chair he was sitting in hit the floor; I heard him yell the words "Oh, no!" and I heard some stumbling around. My first thought was *heart attack!* I rushed up to the kitchen to find

Jimmy leaning over the sink, his glasses off, trying to wash his eyes out with running water. He didn't have to tell me what had happened because the minute I entered the kitchen area I could feel the pepper spray stinging my eyes and my lungs and I began to cough.

There we were—two completely incapacitated people trying to help each other. He couldn't see and I couldn't stop coughing. I managed to pull him out of the area and get him to the back of the house where I could breathe and we could begin washing his face and eyes. Water and time eventually helped us both.

Life is like that sometimes...the unexpected hits us right in the face...clear out of the blue before we've even had time to begin the day with God! I'm so glad He doesn't depend on me to be faithful! I'm so glad that I can know that every minute of every day I am covered by His love, sheltered in the shadow of His wings, grounded on the Rock that is higher than I. He is there ahead of me, in those rude awakenings. He is there waiting to walk with me through tough days. He is faithful even when I am faithless!

Judy Williams

*He guides me in paths of righteousness
for His name's sake.*

Psalm 23:3

CHAPTER TWENTY EIGHT

The Ding in the Car

Doing The Right Thing Even When You Don't Want To

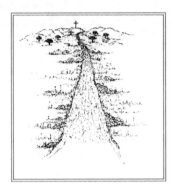

I pulled up in the parking lot next to an old, dilapidated, dirty car. The wind was blowing fiercely that morning and as I opened my driver's side door, the wind caught it and banged it into that old car. I got out, closed my door and looked at the other car. Yes, there was a definite "ding" in the other car's side which had been caused by my door. I knew it was "my" ding because the dirt was knocked off the car in that one spot.

What to do? My mind began to rationalize; to justify. "They won't even notice one more "ding" among all the others on that dirty old car. They don't care about the car anyway, otherwise they would wash it, or at least clean up the inside. Well, I could just put some money on the front seat and write them a note about what happened (to assuage my guilt) and let them be surprised when they come back."

This last thought I decided to put into action, but the car door was locked. I realized they must care something about the car. Now I began to think of legal issues, and my mind went wild: "What if they got angry about the 'ding?' What if they wanted to call insurance companies? What if they weren't happy about what the insurance company wanted to pay?"

Now, I REALLY wanted to walk away as if nothing had happened—maybe even take my car and drive away. As a compromise I decided I would go into the store and glance out once in a while to see if anyone went to the car. If no one had moved the car before I was finished shopping, I would decide what to do then.

I followed this plan and, after completing my shopping, I returned to my car. The old, dilapidated, dirty car was still next to mine. I pushed my buggy to my trunk, unloaded my groceries, pushed my buggy to the buggy container and was walking back to my car when I saw her. She was a young, college-age girl, pushing her buggy straight to "the" car. Now was the moment of decision: To do or not to do the right thing. I didn't want to talk with her. I was apprehensive. I wanted to get in my car and drive away without saying a word. I did not want to do the right thing.

But I knew I must. I went to her, exchanged some pleasantries, then walked her over to the damaged side of her car and showed her what I had done. I told her how sorry I was and offered to pay for the damage.

"No, no," she said. "It's ok. Think nothing of it. I am just so amazed that you waited to tell me about this. You've just helped to remind me there are still good people in this world. You have made my day. Please don't worry any more about it." And, she refused to take any money from me.

Sometimes it is very difficult to do the right thing. Sometimes we don't want to do the right thing. We rationalize, justify, and offer all kinds of excuses about why we don't need to do what we know we should do. When we keep our eyes on Jesus we can hear His whispering behind us, "This is the path of righteousness, walk in it."

Judy Williams

*May the words of my mouth and the meditation of my heart
be pleasing in your sight,
O Lord, my Rock, and my Redeemer.*

Psalm 19:14

CHAPTER TWENTY NINE

Fifteen Minutes of Fame

Hold Onto Your Principles

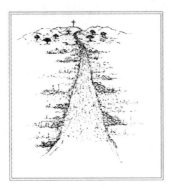

I try to always look my best. I don't always succeed, but I try. I tell people it's in my DNA to look my best at all times. A few years ago I realized I got a little beyond the norm in this desire when I spent a weekend with girlfriends. The first morning I got up and did my ritual of getting dressed, putting on my make-up and fixing my hair. When I got to the kitchen for breakfast there were all my friends still in their pajamas with no make-up on and hair sticking out in all directions. *They* looked at *me* like *I* was the freaky one.

Many years ago, I noticed that some people can be easily distracted from listening. Minor things such as the speaker having smeared lipstick, or wearing two different colored shoes, may cause a listener's mind to wander. One day a woman came into my office and she was carrying on a one-sided conversation with me because I couldn't *hear* a word she was saying. I was distracted because I was focused on her hair. She had forgotten to comb it and although she had taken her rollers out, she had little round, empty curls all over her head.

This experience reaffirmed my feeling that if people were going to listen to what I have to say, I didn't want them to be distracted by some fault in my appearance. I admit this is a flawed and incorrect vision to have and I still work to correct it.

However, keeping the importance of this flawed characteristic of mine in mind, I will tell you how I missed my "Fifteen Minutes of Fame." Jimmy and I had rented a condo on the Isle of Palms in South Carolina for a weekend. Unfortunately, a tropical storm had made its appearance off the coast right in time for our getaway. As Jimmy and I arrived and throughout the night, the winds howled, the rain poured, the surf pounded. We awoke the next morning to a still-ominous sky and weather report.

We decided to walk down to the beach during one of the slight lulls in the weather, but I had failed to bring any rain gear. Jimmy, always prepared like the Boy Scout he was as a child, had not only brought his rain suit, but had something I could wear also. He handed me a poncho that would have fit the Jolly Green Giant. Three people could have fit into the poncho which hung six inches off my hands and dangled around my ankles. He then handed me a bungee cord to wrap around my waist and cinch up my "rain suit" a little. As I walked out onto the streets of the Isle of Palms heading for the beach, I must have resembled an old, tired monk.

The wind and rain quickly whipped the hood around my head and face so that my hair became soaked and plastered to my head. Now add "drowned rat" to the image of the monk.

We were just about to enter the path that led over the sand dunes to the ocean when a white van pulled up beside us and parked. Out of the back of the van emerged a virtual Miss America…a lovely young woman dressed in a beautiful rain coat belted at the waist, crisp lapels, a matching umbrella held over her head. She was a vision of perfection on this gloomy day. Imagine my surprise when she and the young man who was with her walked straight up to Jimmy and me.

126

It was at that moment I noticed a microphone in her hand and a camera on the shoulder of her associate. She talked with us for a few moments, asking us where we were from, how long we planned to stay, what we thought about the stormy weather and how was it affecting our trip. Then she asked, "Would you mind if I interview you for our news program? You'll be on TV tonight."

Remember how important it is to me to always look my best... remember the drowned rat/monk look I am currently sporting and then picture the impeccably attired young woman I would be standing next to. But this is a moment few people have – to be on TV! I hesitate. Then I say, "No, I can't be on TV looking like this."

"But," Miss Perfect replied, "Look how far away you are from home. No one here knows you." That was the challenging statement: I was away from everyone I knew, everyone who knew me. I could be on TV looking like a drowned monk/rat and no one would ever know.

How many times has that thought entered our minds: "No one will ever know, I can commit this one sin, tell this one lie, go this different way, and no one will ever know?"

This experience reminded me to Whom I belong. We are God's ambassadors. We have a responsibility to walk His path of righteousness and be His example of love and goodness and grace, mercy and understanding and forgiveness to the world. If we compromise in one small area of our lives, how easy it is to do so again.

It is important to me to always try to look my best. I would not compromise that principle for anyone. It is important for me to always be God's ambassador to the world. I will not compromise that responsibility. My Heavenly Father has never compromised anything for me. He gave it all – His Only Begotten Son. May I never, never forget to Whom I belong.

I will sing to the Lord all my life;
I will sing praise to my God as long as I live.
May my meditation be pleasing to Him,
as I rejoice in the Lord.

Psalm 104:33,34

CHAPTER THIRTY

The Leviathan Will Frolic

Daily Set Aside Time To Be With God

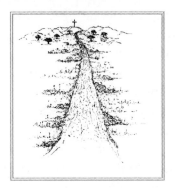

One day Jimmy and I were at Edisto Beach by ourselves; it was March and not a time when many people want to go to the beach. We have a 21 foot bay boat which we like to take out fishing; sometimes we go to a fishing spot eight miles off shore and other times we go out about twenty miles. I'm always a little nervous going out because we are really novices in the scheme of being "captains" of "ships" on the ocean. We've learned some things over the last few years, but there's a lot we don't know.

Keeping our inexperience in mind, I always pray extra hard when I know we're going out on that endless, bottomless sea. On this particular day I read my devotional and prayed while Jimmy was getting the boat ready. That day my reading included the 104th Psalm which speaks about God's creation, the beauty of all

His creation and how He takes care of it. In my reading I came to verses 25 and 26: (Now remember, we are about to go out on the ocean!)

> *There is the sea, vast and spacious, teeming with creatures beyond number – living things both large and small. There the ships go to and fro, and the leviathan which you formed to frolic there.*

"OK, God, I don't fully understand what it is you are telling me, but I'm trusting you because you know where we're going today," I said as I finished my devotional.

The ocean was unusually calm that day, and the water was as slick as glass. We were probably 2 ½ miles off shore and because the water was so calm we could see for a great distance. Jimmy noticed something floating on the water to our left and about parallel with us—maybe a half mile away. I mentioned it might be an overturned boat, but when we got closer to it Jimmy said "I think it's a whale." And that's exactly what it was: a Wright Whale, about 2 ½ times longer than our boat. He came up, he went down. He looked at us with his great big eye and waved at us with his tail. We followed, watched and admired the whale for 45 minutes and then we went on out to our fishing spot. He followed us out, then left to continue his journey into the vast reaches of God's ocean world.

At the end of the day I was considering what an exciting adventure Jimmy and I had experienced ...then, I seemed to hear God laughing as He said to me, "I told you this morning you would 'frolic with my leviathan'." God will tell you great and mighty things you cannot imagine when you read His Word. We need to read it daily, read it intently, and listen for His voice.

Part V
INSPIRATION AND EXAMPLES ALL AROUND US

For the beauty of the earth,
For the glory of the skies,
For the love which from my birth
Over and around me lies,
Lord of all to Thee I raise
This my hymn of grateful praise.

The love of our amazing God is all around us, inspiring witnesses both in this earthly world and in the eternal world to point us toward the Path of Righteousness. They encourage and support us, counsel and comfort us, helping us to keep our eyes on Jesus—the author and perfecter of our faith.

*Therefore, since we are surrounded by such a great cloud of witnesses,
let us throw off everything that hinders
and the sin that so easily entangles,
and let us run with perseverance the race marked out for us.
Let us fix our eyes on Jesus, the author and perfecter of our faith.*

Hebrews 12:1-2b

CHAPTER THIRTY ONE

Mom

An Expression Of Love

Mom was on a trip to Branson, Missouri with her friends. Dad had died a year earlier and this was one of the first times Mom had really gotten out to enjoy life again. She called me from Branson, and I could tell immediately she was in distress. She was in the emergency room of the Branson Hospital with a severe eye infection. In fact, she had an ulcer on her eye that prevented her from wearing her contact lens, so she was practically blind since the ulcer was affecting the only eye she had. Her right eye had been lost in a car accident years earlier.

Mom said she would ride home with the group on the bus but she wanted me to meet her when she arrived in Valdosta to take her to the hospital. Of course I agreed, and I was praying her eye would be ok when she arrived. It was not, and she was admitted to the hospital. Over the next couple of days, tests were run and her physician decided she needed to go to Emory Hospital. To complicate matters, her doctor had seen some suspicious spots on her lungs a few weeks earlier and he wanted a biopsy done as soon as possible.

The physician at Emory wanted to treat Mom for several weeks but did not want to admit her to the hospital, so we came to my home in Athens, Georgia. Since she would be staying with me at least several weeks, we secured a physician in Athens to investigate her suspicious lung problem.

A week later a biopsy was scheduled and I took her to the hospital. I prayed as I waited for the procedure to be finished and the results known. As the doctor approached me from the surgical room, I could tell he was in a hurry. He told me the results were not good. My mother had terminal lung cancer.

"When are you going to tell her?" I asked.

He told me it would be some time the next week before he could see her, as he was on his way to another surgery at this time and it would be a while before Mom was awake. "I would like for you to tell her," he said. "It is usually easier to hear this kind of news from someone who loves you."

Wow. Just like that, I felt the burden of the world descend upon my shoulders. Not just telling Mom the results, but the realization of what the results meant for her and for me and for all who loved her, brought an overwhelming heaviness to my heart. I sat and waited for Mom to be rolled out. I may have prayed…I don't remember; I may have planned some words to say to her…I don't remember. What I do remember is sitting in that lonely chair, in that empty corridor, stunned. Then I saw the nurses rolling her bed out of the operating room.

She was still a little sleepy, but she looked at me and smiled. "I don't guess they found anything, did they?" she asked.

As I looked back at her, the tears began to roll down my cheeks. "Yes, Mom, they did." I replied. "It isn't good news." Then I began to sob uncontrollably.

She reached up her arms and wrapped me in her love and whispered in my ear, "It's ok, Judy. It's going to be alright."

She comforted me. After hearing the worst news anyone wants to hear, my mother comforted me. During the next few months as the cancer grew and consumed her body, she continued to be a source of joy in my home. Despite the fact she could barely see (her eye never improved), despite the fact she was far from her home and her friends, and she was dying of cancer, my mother lifted me up every day. She never complained, she was never anxious, she never cried or had a pity party. She planned her funeral. She was not only an inspiring witness to me, she is in my cloud of witnesses continuing to encourage me.

Our God is the "Father of compassion and the God of all comfort who comforts us in all our troubles, so that we can comfort those in any trouble with the comfort we ourselves have received from God" (II Corinthians 1:3, 4). I remember those days of God using my mother to comfort me. As a Stephen Minister, a one-on-one Christian care-giving ministry, I use memories like this one of my mother to bring to others the care and compassion of our loving Heavenly Father.

You are the light of the world.

Matthew5:14a

CHAPTER THIRTY TWO

Light of My Life

Don't Put Your Light Under A Basket

*I*t was a beautiful late spring day. I was walking with our grandsons down the driveway and heading for the kitchen for snacks after a full school day. Six year old Hunter was full of energy and excitement telling me about his day. Ten year old Logan was unusually quiet and thoughtful. He kicked the gravel rocks along the driveway, gave the fire ant hills a quick stomp as we walked along. But, he didn't say a word.

I tried to get Logan to talk while listening and responding to Hunter, but Logan remained silent. Finally, just before we reached the house he looked at me and asked, "Grammy, you know what?"

"What?" I questioned.

"You're the light of my life," he said.

Time stopped still for me. What did Logan just say? 'I' am the light of his life? What a gift; what an honor; what a *responsibility*! My mind spun with these and other thoughts at what he had just said.

I was amazed at the depth of these words thought out and spoken by a 10 year old boy. And I thought about Christ who has told me, "you are the light of the world." That's what I was; the Light of Christ to this child. I am Christ's light to Logan. I am Christ's example not only to Logan but to all whom I meet. I am Christ's Light to the world, to my family, my friends, and strangers. I am His Light. Logan opened my eyes to this truth on that afternoon.

We, God's chosen, the Body of Christ, Christians, are called to be the light of Christ to this hurting world. Logan is one of my inspiring witnesses. I hear God whisper to me through him, "The closer you walk to the Light, the brighter you will become. You are my light in this dark world."

Judy Williams

Children's children are a crown to the aged....

Proverbs 17:6a

CHAPTER THIRTY THREE

A Sliver of Moon

One Of The Ways We Learn

*I*t was a bright, starry night in the city of Atlanta. That sounds a little strange, doesn't it? Who can ever see the stars when looking into the skies above Atlanta? But for some reason this night was different. It was the middle of summer and the sky was exceptionally black and the stars exceptionally bright.

Hanging in the middle of that blackness surrounded by a twinkling of stars was a sliver of moon, thin and white. Mia, our granddaughter, was looking out the window of the car as we drove through the streets looking for a restaurant. She was the first to notice the splendor of God's glory above us and she called our attention to something we might have missed, "Look, Grammy," she said, "it's God's fingernail." She was referring to the sliver of moon in the sky.

"Is that right?" I responded to her.

"Yes," she answered, "that's what Mom has always told us.

When the moon looks like that, it's God's fingernail."

Then I told Mia, "And that's what I told your mother when she was a little girl. That's also how my mother, your great-grandmother, described the moon to me when it looked like this. And your great-grandmother learned that description from her mother."

Someday Mia will pass this well-known truth along to her children. And she will tell where she learned it as she repeats it to her children. It's one of the ways we learn about ourselves, about our families, and about our God. "Train up a child in the way he should go, and when he is grown he will not depart from it." Proverbs 22:6 Children listen to parents even when we do not know they are listening.

Judy Williams

Even though I walk through the valley of the shadow of death,
I will fear no evil, for you are with me;
Your rod and Your staff they comfort me.
You prepare a table before me in the presence of my enemies.
You anoint my head with oil; my cup overflows.
Surely goodness and love will follow me all the days of my life,
and I will dwell in the house of the Lord forever.

Psalm 23:4-6

CHAPTER THIRTY FOUR

Moving Forward

Blessed To Be A Blessing

A few years ago, I talked with a good friend who had lost a child through a tragic accident. The years have come and gone since that tragedy. Don't think for a minute she does not still grieve. She does, she will never stop grieving. But there is such joy on the face of this woman, and she is a joy to be around. She blesses the lives of everyone who knows her in so many ways.

In my conversation with her that day, I questioned her about the fact that she has moved on with her life, been able to move beyond such a great tragedy and heartache. How had she been able to do it? She said to me the most wonderful thing: "I chose to live for my family who are still here. I knew in those first days and months that I could sink, and I knew I had a choice to make." She chose life.

Not only in these years since her son's death has my friend been a blessing to others, she has been blessed by God. She's one of my inspiring witnesses. When I am going through rough times and don't think I can make it, I hear my Heavenly Father speaking to me through my inspiring friend as He says, "Choose life, Judy, choose life." And I know He is walking just ahead of me as I return my focus to Him.

Judy Williams

Now you are the body of Christ,
and each one of you is a part of it.

I Corinthians 12:27

CHAPTER THIRTY FIVE

Selflessness
Putting Others First

Recently in my Sunday school class one of our members, a single, elderly lady, was scheduled to have surgery. I heard another member ask if she could help her with transportation to the hospital and back home after surgery was over. "Wow. No one has ever offered to do anything like that for me before. I'm so used to doing things for myself, I don't know what to say," the elderly lady answered.

As I stood nearby watching and listening to this conversation my only thought was: "Why didn't I think of doing that for her?" It never occurred to me to make such a special offer. I just think of the ordinary things like sending a card, helping to prepare a meal, calling or visiting. Then as I looked at the faces of those two women, I saw Jesus blessing them both. Their faces were expressing compassion, gratitude, mercy and love.

Jesus reminds me daily that I am not supposed to "do it all." That's what the Body of Christ is about, the Church. Each one of us helping the other; building each other up, cheering each other on, reminding us of lessons learned. Each one of us is using his or her uniqueness to build up, support, and encourage the Body of Christ. Now when I become overwhelmed with the busyness of my life I remember the faces of these two women and how our Father in heaven wants to bless each one of us as we uniquely respond to Him and are a blessing to others.

Judy Williams

Morning has broken like the first morning.
Blackbird has spoken like the first bird.
Praise for the singing, praise for the morning
Praise for them springing fresh from the Word.

From **"Morning Has Broken"**
lyrics by **Eleanor Farjeon**

CHAPTER THIRTY SIX

God's Love Is All Around Us

A Lesson From My Husband

I like to see new and different things. For example, the sight of a squirrel scampering in our yard is "old news" to me. I've seen a thousand! Or daffodils each spring. Sure, I enjoy watching them introduce and welcome the new season after a cold winter, but they're yellow every year, year after year.

My husband is not like me. Jimmy awakes every morning looking at all creation as "brand new" as if he has never seen it before. When we're taking our morning walks he will say to me, "Look, Judy, there goes a squirrel," as though he had never seen one before. Or, "A deer's been through here this morning." He may even pick a tiny wild flower and examine it, or pick up an unusual rock and take it home. We have rocks all over our house with no idea from where they came.

On our walks, my eyes are usually on the road or path in front of me; my mind a million different places…but not Jimmy's. His eyes will see the beautiful red-tailed hawk flying above the trees

153

looking for a meal. He will see the beautiful, meticulously crafted hornets' nest hanging in the cedar tree. He will smell the fragrance of the fresh honeysuckle. He will detect the new fruit beginning to form on the pear tree. And he will point it all out to me.

He loves to "explore." Many, many times on trips, we have taken back roads because the view is more scenic. We will hike different paths to "see what we can see." Or just walk around our property looking and exploring. A few years ago Jimmy wanted to get a boat to take out in the ocean at Edisto. He wanted to explore the creeks and inlets and learn all he could about the ocean and the marshes and how to fish and enjoy them. And, in all this, he again opened my eyes to the beauty of the earth and the glory of the skies. He settles me down to enjoy God's creation every minute of every day, just as he does.

Jimmy's perspective on life is exemplified in his favorite song/hymn "Morning has Broken." Every day, every experience of every day, every thought, plan and action of every day is "brand new" to Jimmy. He reveals to me an example of trusting God with every moment of your life and reaping the bounty of His goodness. What an inspiring witness my husband is.

Judy Williams

But the fruit of the Spirit is love, joy, peace, patience, kindness, goodness, faithfulness, gentleness, and self-control...

Galatians 5:22,23a

CHAPTER THIRTY SEVEN

Being a Member of the Team
Being Where We're Supposed To Be

*O*ne saturday we attended our grandson Gavin's soccer tournament. We got up to leave Columbia, SC around 6:00 a.m. to be in Augusta, GA by 7:30 a.m. It was misty, rainy, and cold. Marie, Gavin's 16 year old sister, probably had other things she wanted to do that day, but she was "encouraged" to go and so she did..

Marie, her mother, Jimmy and I sat on the wet benches in the drizzle wishing the concession stand would hurry up and open so we could get some coffee or hot chocolate. About halfway through the game, I looked over at Marie. She was wearing her Daddy's jacket so she could be warmer, the lower half of her face was wrapped up in a wooly scarf, hat on her head, mittens on her hands, feet tucked up under her. She wasn't saying much. None of us was. It was a miserable, cold and wet day.

Then, out of the blue Marie said, "You know what? I feel so

157

good! I mean, I feel really happy! I don't understand why I feel this way, I'm cold and wet and miserable, but I feel so happy!"

What an unusual declaration in the midst of not being where you want to be, watching your little brother's soccer game in the cold and wet, trying to stay warm and feeling cold and miserable, but feeling happy and good at the same time. I know why Marie felt happy and good. She was where she was supposed to be. She was on the family team, supporting her brother. She was where God wanted her to be, on God's team, united with her family and also doing God's will.

We have all been in places where we are cold and miserable on the outside, in our physical world, but in those cold and miserable places, we can be happy and feel good on the inside, in God's world, in God's will. Whenever we are where we are supposed to be, doing what we are supposed to do, being who God created us to be we are enthusiastic, happy, productive and fulfilled. Every time!!!

Judy Williams

> *...without the shedding of blood*
> *there is no forgiveness.*
>
> **Hebrews 9:22b**

CHAPTER THIRTY EIGHT

Dumb Turkeys

An Interesting Way To Learn The Truth

I have always heard stories about turkeys being dumb. Stories such as: turkeys don't know when to take their heads out of a deep water bucket when they're drinking, so they drown. Or: turkeys peck each other to death if they see blood on another turkey. Big fights then ensue and lots of turkeys die.

Actually the second story is a fact: a turkey will peck another to death while trying to remove a blemish or wound. This was a terrible problem for turkey farmers, so when someone developed goggles to put on turkeys to prevent them from pecking each other to death, turkey farmers gobbled up the goggles (pun intended!). Now all the turkeys on a turkey farm are fitted with tiny red goggles, and when they look through these goggles all they see are red turkeys with no wounds. What an amazing adaptation.

Our Heavenly Father was the first to think of the solution to a serious problem. He looks at us through "red goggles." He looks at us through the blood of Jesus, His Only Begotten Son, and He sees us as perfect. He sees us wrapped in the righteousness of Jesus, cleansed by His blood, and we are able stand before the Father. We are able to come into His very presence and worship Him. Now THAT'S amazing. That's GRACE.

Judy Williams

It was [God] who gave [gifts]…
to prepare God's people for works of service,
so that the body of Christ may be built up
until we all reach unity in the faith
and in the knowledge of the Son of God
and become mature,
attaining to the whole measure of the fullness of Christ.

Ephesians 4:11a; 12-13

CHAPTER THIRTY NINE

The Servant

We All Have Special Gifts From God

*B*efore relating this story, I must first mention the importance of knowing and using our Spiritual Gifts. Each and every one of us has been uniquely endowed with certain spiritual gifts. (See Romans 12:6-8; I Corinthians 12:8-10, 28; Ephesians 4:11). These are not gifts we earn or even deserve, they are simply gifts from God, and they are to be used to build up the Body of Christ, the Church, the people of God. They are to be used by the Body of Christ to bring hope and healing to this hurting world. One of those gifts is serving.

My mother had been diagnosed with lung cancer. She had only a short time to live. Complicating her situation was the fact that she was not only visually impaired as a result of losing an eye in an automobile accident when she was a young woman, she now had an ulcer on her remaining eye. Her vision in her last days was very limited. She had come to visit me and during that visit two diagnoses had been made: she would not ever see clearly again, and she was dying with lung cancer. She would stay with me until God called her home.

Since my husband and I were both still working, we needed to find someone who could help us care for Mother during the day. I immediately thought of my friend, Kathryn. Kathryn is the type of person who puts her whole self into anything she takes on. She is a most compassionate, understanding and capable person. I gave Kathryn a call and she agreed to help out for a few days to see how things went.

From the moment Kathryn and my mother met, there was a bonding which developed into a great friendship. In those first days Kathryn and Mother had lots of fun getting to know each other. They would sit in our rocking chairs on the screened in back porch and visit and laugh for hours. After a couple of weeks, in order to make my life more simple, Kathryn took over cleaning my house and preparing a wonderful dinner for our family in the evenings. She would never stay to eat with us...always telling me this was a time our family needed to be together.

One morning Mother rolled over in bed and broke her hip. The cancer had spread to her bones. Surgery was required and when we brought Mother home from the hospital, Kathryn was waiting with arms open wide to help Mother in whatever way she needed. Mother's activities were now much more restricted.

As the weeks passed, Mother became more confined to her bed. Whenever Mother wanted to get up, Kathryn would help her into her wheelchair and push her out on the porch, or around the yard, or they would just sit and visit in the den. The moment she had mother settled, Kathryn would hurry back to Mother's bedroom and re-make her bed, taking her satin pillowcase off the pillow, folding it and placing it in the freezer. When she saw that Mother was ready to return to her bedroom to rest awhile, Kathryn went to the freezer and removed the pillowcase. She put the cooled pillowcase on the pillow and turned down Mother's bed, so Mother always got into a fresh bed and lay her head on a cool pillowcase. It did not matter if Mother was out of the bed ten minutes or two hours; this procedure was always the same.

As the end of Mother's life drew near, Kathryn was at her bedside whenever I could not be home. On the day of Mother's death, my sister Julie, my daughter Ashley and I were beside her. Julie, Ashley and I sang hymns to Mother. We prayed together. We held her hands as she slipped into the arms of Jesus. Kathryn had left the house for a short while and when she returned I told her that Mother had died. She asked if she could spend a few minutes alone with her.

Kathryn went into Mother's room and closed the door. A little while later she came out and asked Julie and me to go in. There I saw Kathryn's final gift to my mother, and her gift for me. Kathryn had bathed Mother; fixed her hair, put on her makeup, and dressed her in a beautiful white gown which she had purchased for Mother. My Mother looked like an angel. She was truly at peace and free of pain as she rested in the arms of Jesus. She was beautiful.

When we are using the spiritual gifts that God has given us, we go beyond what is required of us. We go beyond what we can think or imagine because we are being guided by God. We are doing His work for His children. When we use our gifts to build up the Body of Christ, to minister to His children, not only are others blessed, *we* are blessed. We know we are doing His work because we have such joy in our task. Kathryn was God's servant to my mother. Not only was Kathryn a blessing to my mother and to all of my family, she was blessed by God as she did His work.

Kathryn, my dear friend, servant of God, died recently. I had the privilege of telling "her" story at her memorial service.

I remember the days of long ago;
I meditate on all your works
and consider what your hands have done.

Psalm 143:5

CHAPTER FORTY

The Red Gown

A Moment Of Déjà Vu

Our granddaughter Megan had been invited to the Senior Prom. Her dress had been ordered, sized and fitted perfectly. Matching shoes had been bought along with coordinating jewelry. The corsage and boutonnière were to be picked up on Saturday morning. I had been invited to come over and share in the experience of watching Megan prepare for this important event in her life.

I arrived early Saturday because it would be a day full of activities. The first thing Megan told me as I opened the door was that her gown did not fit. Apparently she had gained a couple of pounds and the zipper would no longer stay closed. So, one additional activity had been added to the list for the day...we would look for another dress. The dress had to be red so that all of the accessories would match.

We began the day by keeping appointments for manicures and

pedicures for Megan, her mother Tracy, her sister Mia and me. I remembered the day of my senior prom many years before, when I got up early and painted my fingernails and toenails, wanting them to be just perfect for the evening and my date with my steady boyfriend.

From the nail salon we went to the beauty parlor. Megan's long dark tresses had recently been cut and styled into a beautiful short haircut. This morning, the hair stylist was waiting for her, to trim her hair to perfection. He was as excited as all of us were about the important evening ahead. On the day of my prom I washed my hair early and then rolled it with big brush rollers. I let the rollers stay in all day hoping the curls would remain for the whole evening.

Now it was time for a quick lunch and then on to shop for a dress. Megan knew the store she wanted because she had been there previously and had seen and tried on a dress she thought would work, if it were still available. It was, and in my opinion, this dress was even more beautiful than the custom made one. It was a very figure enhancing, long, and slim red dress with a one-shoulder strap. Megan is 5'11" and weighs 110 pounds and she absolutely looked like a model in this red dress.

I remembered my prom dress. It was the most beautiful dress I had ever seen: strapless, white, with glittering bands of silver through the bodice and skirt. It was full with several petticoats and hoops under it. I felt like a true Southern Belle when I put it on.

Megan's date arrived promptly at seven that evening. She glided down the stairway like the model she is to meet him. She was beautiful in her red gown, all accessories matching. He slipped the red corsage on her wrist and she pinned the boutonnière on his lapel. He was delighted that he was an inch taller than she despite her spike heels. The cameras flashed and the couple were gone for an evening of making memories.

All throughout the day, I had remembered my prom evening of years before: the beautiful dress, the tiara on my head, the sparkling earrings, the white orchid on my wrist. How I enjoyed taking a walk down memory lane through participating in my granddaughter's prom day. This was a moment of déjà vu.

We all have good memories. God had given us wonderful minds to recall good and happy times. Our ability to recall is one of His best gifts. He tells us to recall often, "remember when..." It's one of the ways He brings a smile to our faces and love again into our hearts.

Often when I am writing a note to someone who is in a crisis situation or who has lost a loved one I will tell them I am praying for God to bring to their memory wonderful experiences they have shared with their loved one so that they can relive those moments again, so that they can experience the joy and happiness they felt in those initial experiences once more. In all of the special days in our lives He wants us to remember Him. He is present with us always, laughing and enjoying whatever brings us happiness. The joy of the Lord is my strength (in my day of trouble).

"*For my thoughts are not your thoughts,*
neither are your ways my ways," declares the Lord.
"*As the heavens are higher than the earth,*
so are my ways higher than your ways
and my thoughts than your thoughts."

Isaiah 55:8,9

CHAPTER FORTY ONE

The BB Gun

Keep Your Focus

*E*ight year old Jimmy was at our house one day and Papa was teaching him how to shoot the BB gun. He practiced loading the gun and holding it safely. He learned how to stand with his side to the target (a group of tin cans) and how to balance the gun. He learned how to close one eye, aim down the barrel, and squeeze the trigger.

He did very well hitting the target nearly every time, as long as Papa was beside him. Then Papa went inside and Jimmy was on his own. Wow, did he feel big and independent! Jimmy remembered everything Papa had taught him. He made sure the gun was loaded, always holding it safely and properly. He turned his side to the target, raised the gun, sighted down the barrel at the tin cans and slowly pulled the trigger. Not a single can fell down.

Jimmy couldn't believe it! He went through his steps again, one by one, making sure to do everything Papa had said. He pulled the trigger once again and still no cans hit the dirt. What was the matter? He moved a few steps closer to the cans, proceeded as before, and again pulled the trigger. Still no results. He went through the process one more time moving a few steps closer, but still no cans fell.

I could see his little mind racing as I watched him out the kitchen window. "To heck with this!" he must have thought as he walked over to the cans and, with the barrel of the gun, pushed each can over. Then he threw the rifle over his shoulder and walked into the house.

This story reminds me of my prayer life sometimes. I will have a prayer need or request for God and I can already see the answer, my answer. I can see the results of my request as clearly as Jimmy could see the results of his shooting the BB gun—the cans would fall. I have done everything I know to do about this prayer request as I've prayed to God and sought His will.

My problem comes when I don't see the results I am expecting, and I may walk over and push the cans down thinking, "God needs a little help." Most of the time my taking matters into my own hands to be sure I get the results I want ends in disaster. However, if after praying and searching the scriptures I truly seek God's will and put the results (whatever they may be) in His hands I am filled with His peace. When I remember God's thoughts are not my thoughts, and His ways are not my ways; when I remember His thoughts and His ways are so much better than anything I could think or imagine, then I am filled with His peace as I await His answers to my prayers.

Judy Williams

This is good, and pleases God our Savior,
who wants all men to be saved
and to come to a knowledge of the truth.

I Timothy 2:3,4

CHAPTER FORTY TWO

Don't Be Afraid to Let Go

The Influence Of The World

*B*ecause we live so close to the "chicken capital of the world," Gainesville, Georgia, we have seen a lot of chicken trucks packed with caged chickens barreling down our local roadways. I have often wondered how those chickens that are locked in the middle confines of the truck can even breathe.

One day I was traveling alongside one of those chicken-laden trucks and I happened to look up and on top of the truck was a lone chicken who had managed to escape. She was not a happy girl. Her hair feathers were slicked back from the wind and full of dust and dirt, her beak gritted and encrusted with bugs, her eyes squinted almost shut. She was holding on to the bars of her now vacant cage for dear life. She wanted to be back in her cage beside her friends.

And her friends were urging her to come back in, trying to help her come back to the fellowship, the friendship of her old way of

177

life. Reminding her how much better and safer it was inside the cage. There was a part of her that wanted to go back inside. But, a part of her realized that she was free. She had a chance at a new life and all she had to do was let go and fly.

Where was that chicken truck heading? To the processing plant in Gainesville, Georgia. To the slaughter house. To destruction. If that chicken scrabbled back to the comfort and security of being inside the truck with her friends, she was headed for trouble. If she let go of the cage top, she had an opportunity for new life. She had a choice to make. We all have that choice to make: to return to the pathway that leads to destruction, the path of old friends, worldly security, familiarity; or to let go of our old ways and follow the path which leads to life.

Daily I need to climb down off the chicken truck; let go of my old ways; listen to the One who loves me more than anyone else, my Lord and Savior. I need to "hang on tight" to the Shepherd and Guardian of my soul, Jesus Christ.

Judy Williams

> *He guides me in paths of righteousness*
> *For His Name's sake.*
> *Psalm 23:3*
> *Every good and perfect gift is from above..*
>
> **James 1:17**

CHAPTER FORTY THREE

Temptation

It Waits For Us

Jimmy and I had just finished washing the windows of our sunroom. This is one of those jobs which I find not only tedious, but messy, and one which strains my arms beyond their endurance and causes my neck to bend at unforgiving angles. But now the job was done, and, Jimmy and I were enjoying the beautiful, clean, unobstructed view out the windows.

The day was beautiful...sun shining on our lush green lawn, azaleas in full bloom, trees with their multiple colors of green, and the glistening lake looking like a field of diamonds. As I looked through the windows, the view was so clear that it appeared there was no barrier between me and what I saw beyond. Then something caught my eye.

Floating on the gentle breeze was what looked like a long iridescent thread. It waved and undulated through the air with no apparent beginning or end. It was beautiful with its multiple colors. Within a few minutes I saw several more threads, then many more, their "anchor" seemed to be the big oak tree at the edge of our yard.

The threads appeared to be tangled as they waved and floated, boasting their colors. It was a beautiful display...but I knew what they were. At the end of each lovely, iridescent thread was a very tiny spider moving away from home for the first time. Each spider wanted to attach his thread to a stable foundation...something he could build on to spin his web.

As I looked at these threads waving in the sunlight, there appeared to be no "danger" in them. However, I knew it would not be long before dust and bugs and grit and grime would attach to the sticky spider threads. It wouldn't be long before my view of the outside world would be obstructed once again.

I think that's the way temptation is to us a lot of the time. It's beautiful, or righteous, or justified. And when we allow one small thread to attach itself to us—when we yield to temptation—then it's not long before things that are not so pretty, the dirt and grime—the sin—in our lives begins to obstruct the windows of our souls. We begin to lose our view of the path ahead of us. The path on which Jesus leads us. The path of Righteousness.

Satan tempted Eve through what was "good for food, pleasing to the eye, and desirable for gaining wisdom." All things which are "beautiful." To walk the path of righteousness, we must follow the One who leads us on the path of Righteousness...Our Shepherd. Then all these things (which are right and beautiful) will be given to us.

Judy Williams

For the joy of the Lord is my strength.

Nehemiah 8:10

CHAPTER FORTY FOUR

The Bully

When God Is For Us, Who Can Be Against Us

Our youngest grandson, Jimmy, is small for his age. He is also not heavily involved in sports, although he does love to play football and soccer and has taken some karate lessons. Jimmy's biggest interest is Hip Hop Dancing.

This type of dancing involves a lot of acrobatics and strength-bearing moves and Jimmy is very good at it. A couple of years ago he was the only boy who tried out for the dance program at school and of course he was eagerly received by the instructor. In the past few months he has joined a community hip hop dance company being one of a few out of hundreds chosen to participate.

For these two reasons—his small stature and his love of dancing—I believe Jimmy has been a victim of bullying. He went to his parents several months ago to talk with them about a problem he was having with some bigger boys at school. These facts alone have impressed me: that he was comfortable enough in his relationship with his parents and could share with them the problem he was encountering, and his parents were willing to listen and then to give good advice. This speaks to me of an excellent parent/ child relationship.

After Jimmy explained his problem to his parents—a group of boys were making him the center of unwanted, negative attention—he told them he wanted to handle the situation on his own. Phil and Tracy gave him this advice: 1) Talk first with the counselor at school so she would know what was occurring just in case the meeting with his primary "opponent" went badly; and 2) Be sure to meet with the boy one-on-one. None of his friends nor his opponents should be around.

Jimmy followed the advice of his parents by going first to the counselor, explaining the problem, and then telling her his plans about handling it on his own. She asked him to come to her after it was over and let her know the results. Within a few days Jimmy had the opportunity to meet with the boy alone and he said to him, "I don't appreciate the way you have been treating me and I want it to stop." The boy, with none of his "supporters" around, was clearly flustered. All he said was, "O.K." There have been no more bullying problems with this boy or the other members of his group since that time.

In March of 2013, Jimmy was confirmed at his church. He not only joined the church, but he also gave his life to Jesus and accepted Him as his Lord and Savior. In the experience I have just related Jimmy obviously depended on His Savior from beginning to end...not only going to those people responsible for him and for his safety (his parents, the school counselor), but listening to and applying their advice. He also sought the wisdom of God in the words he would say and the time and place he would meet with the boy. Oh, that we all would turn so promptly to the Lord in our day of trouble.

Judy Williams

*For God did not give us a spirit of timidity,
but a spirit of power, of love and of self-discipline.*

II Timothy 1:7

CHAPTER FORTY FIVE

A Home away from Home

God Knows Where His Children Are

We were planning a large brunch at our house which would take place in the yard. In preparation for the event I wanted to replace the well-worn and stained curtains hanging in the garage windows with an updated window treatment: wooden blinds. A nest of wrens complicated my making this change because mother wren had built her cocoon style home between the old curtain and one of the windows. As the date for the brunch drew near, I kept watch on the young family, hoping they would fly away soon.

The day before the occasion, I peeped into the nest, and was delighted to see that it was empty. I asked Jimmy to move the vacated nest to a new location in a dry grapevine wreath that hung on an opposite wall of the garage. The nest was flimsy and he carefully placed it in the vines. When he turned to leave he heard little "tweets" coming from deep inside the leaves and moss. The baby birds were still inside.

We didn't know what to do because we had always heard that if a person touches a nest or an egg or a baby bird, the mother will abandon it all. So we left the young family in the wreath. I was working in the garage and a few minutes later I saw *mama* fly in, looking around the window for her home and her babies. I went to find Jimmy and asked him to put the nest back in the window. Handling the nest even more carefully this time, he returned it to its original setting.

I continued to work in the garage and it wasn't long before I noticed mother bird coming in again and this time she hopped over to the now empty grapevine wreath looking for her babies. I ran to get Jimmy and explained the situation—that the momma bird was searching for her little ones in the wrong place *again*—and I asked him to move the nest back to the dry vines.

Jimmy took the nest once more—now it was completely falling apart—from the window to the wreath. As he gently placed it among the interwoven stems, baby birds began jumping out. He picked the little ones up off the garage floor and put them back in the nest several times. Each time they jumped out again. Finally he gathered them up and crammed them head in, tails out, into the crumbling cocoon.

A little while later mama bird returned to the grapevine nest and began feeding her babies. Over the next several days she fed them continuously and about a week later every one of those little wrens flew from the nest.

When her family and her home were missing, Mama Wren searched for her children and found them. It didn't matter where their nest was moved; she was going to find her babies and care for them no matter what.

No matter where we go our Heavenly Father watches over us, too. If we are uprooted, lost, feeling alone, He is beside us to care for us. If we go to the heavens, He is there; if we make our beds in the depths, He is there. If we rise on the

wings of the dawn, or settle on the far side of the sea, even there His hand will guide us, His right hand will hold us fast (Psalm 139:8-10). There is nowhere we can go that our God will not be there ahead of us waiting to take care of us. What a promise! What an awesome Father!

CONCLUSION

Although this collection of stories has come to an end, I don't believe I will ever stop writing. Every day God continues to reveal Himself to me through memories, experiences, and people, and then He inspires me to write a story about what He has taught me.

A few days ago during the midst of a sleet/ice/snow storm, a very small bird crashed into a window in our sunroom. The bird immediately dropped to the icy ground where he lay for several minutes. We could see him moving slightly and waited for him to gather himself together and fly away. He did not. Finally, Jimmy went outside and picked him up. He handed me this small beautiful creature and as I held him in the palm of my hand, I could feel him centering his little feet under himself.

He was a beautiful dark gray with just a touch of yellow feathering on his breast. He looked at me intently with his dark black eyes, then tucked his little head under his dark gray wing as if he were going to take a nap. Every few seconds he would peep out and look at me then tuck his head under his wing again. Many different messages from God began to fill my thoughts, and then stories began to materialize in my head about what God was teaching me as I held His small creation in the palm of my hand.

This experience is a story yet to be written, as are others. I continue to be delighted and amazed, inspired by God as He teaches me of Himself through the commonplace occurrences of my life.

CPSIA information can be obtained at www.ICGtesting.com
Printed in the USA
LVOW08s1228170914

404456LV00001B/1/P